SQUEEZE PLAY MADE EASY

Books by Terence Reese

Terence Reese has written about 45 books on bridge, poker, canasta and backgammon. These are some of his most important books on bridge:

Begin Bridge with Reese*
Reese on Play
The Expert Game (in America, "Master Play")
Play Bridge with Reese*
Develop Your Bidding Judgment*
Play These Hands with Me
The Bridge Player's Dictionary*
The Blue Club
Precision Bidding and Precision Play*
Bridge at the Top
    with Albert Dormer:
The Complete Book of Bridge
The Play of the Cards
Bridge: The Acol System of Bidding
The Most Puzzling Situations in
    Bridge Play*

Published by Sterling

SQUEEZE PLAY MADE EASY

Techniques for Advanced Bridge Players

Terence Reese & Patrick Jourdain

Sterling Publishing Co., Inc. New York

Contents

Preface by Terence Reese   *page* ix
1. First Principles   1
2. The Simple Squeeze   10
3. Arranging the Menaces   26
4. Arranging the Entries   39
5. Arranging the Timing   49
6. Variations of the Simple Squeeze   59
7. Squeezing Both Opponents   77
8. Two Tricks from a Squeeze   91
9. Pressure in Space   103
10. Exotica   112
11. Defence to Squeeze Play   129

Preface by Terence Reese

When I first wrote some chapters on squeeze play (was it really thirty-two years ago?) I remarked that squeeze play had to be learned – it could not be 'picked up'. I think that is right. It is a knack, not closely related to other skills in the game.

While complex problems can be built around it, squeeze play in its practical aspects is not particularly difficult. It takes time, admittedly. While you may feel, after reading this book, that you understand the technique, you must not expect at first to achieve many successful squeezes at the table. If you return to the book after a period, you will find that you will extract much more from it.

The squeeze is by no means a 'fancy' play. A friend who has good card sense asked me once how often a squeeze really occurred at the table. He was incredulous when I said that squeeze possibilities – not always fulfilled, of course – arose on about one hand in every six or seven. But this is perfectly true, and any good player would say the same.

I have written a number of books dealing with problem hands and for a long while I have known my co-author, Patrick Jourdain, to be the best long-stop in the business – the best protection against those boring people whose letters begin 'Your problem is wrong because . . .' I am therefore especially pleased now to have him bowling at the other end.

SQUEEZE PLAY MADE EASY

1. First Principles

To the novice attending his first bridge class, even the simple finesse is a mystery to be unravelled. Teacher will ask how he will handle x x opposite A Q. After puzzling through the somewhat limited number of choices, the beginner grasps one of the most important principles of play. By leading towards the A Q he profits from the *positional element* in play. If he had to lead from the A Q he would inevitably lose a trick to the King.

When the class begins to play full deals the beginner will soon discover another fact of life. Towards the end of the hand he will find, as a defender, that he cannot retain all the cards he would like to. He will be forced to discard some of his treasures, enabling the declarer to win tricks that originally did not belong to him. The beginner has discovered *pressure in space*.

Another way of describing the same phenomenon is to say that the *combined strength* of declarer and dummy will often prove too much for a single defender. Observe this combination:

♠ A x		♠ K Q x x
♡ K Q x x	opposite	♡ A x
♢ x		♢ x
♣ —		♣ —

If no spades or hearts have been discarded, then evidently the declarer is entitled to only three tricks in each suit. One defender must hold at least four spades and one defender must hold at least four hearts. But suppose the *same* defender has length in both suits: then he will already have been on the rack, forced to unguard one suit or the other. Therein lies the essence of squeeze play.

So our novice, although he may not use such terms, has already discovered the effect of position, of pressure in space, and of combined strength. Position is not always important, but the other two elements are present in every squeeze. All three can be seen in this basic ending:

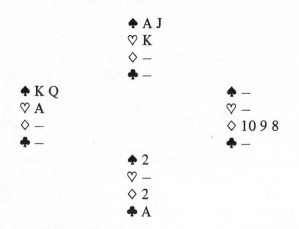

South has only two top winners, but when he plays off ♣ A he forces West to unguard either hearts or spades, establishing a third winner in the dummy. Note here that position is important: if you transfer the East and West cards there is no squeeze, because North has to discard before East.

The simple diagram above contains certain other elements that need to be identified. (Don't be put off by the fact that this section of the book appears to deal with theoretical matters. You *must* grasp underlying theory before you can practise squeeze play, just as you must learn about grip and stance before you can swing a golf club to good effect.)

First, West has two suits to control: that is his dilemma. The cards that threaten him are the Jack of spades and the King of hearts. These cards are called MENACES. Essentially, in every squeeze you must look for *two menace cards lying against the same opponent*.

Second, West is squeezed by a card on which he is unable to follow suit, in this case the Ace of clubs. The Ace of clubs is the SQUEEZE CARD, the one that turns the screw.

Third, there must be communication between declarer and dummy. In the present example the link is in spades. If South had no spade to lead to dummy's A J, then dummy's cards would be useless. Generally speaking (though the criss-cross squeeze and the suicide squeeze, described in later chapters, provide apparent exceptions), there must be an ENTRY to the two-card menace, represented here by ♠ A J.

Fourth, the position must be 'tight'. For the squeeze card to do its job effectively, it must be played at a moment when it exerts real pressure. The victim must not possess any spare card which can be thrown without discomfort. The usual term is no IDLE card; all his cards must be BUSY. To show what is meant, see what happens if you add a superfluous card to the original diagram.

```
                    ♠ A J
                    ♡ K
                    ◇ 4
                    ♣ —
    ♠ K Q                              ♠ —
    ♡ A                               ♡ —
    ◇ 6                               ◇ 10 9 8
    ♣ —                               ♣ 5
                    ♠ 2
                    ♡ —
                    ◇ 3 2
                    ♣ A
```

An extra diamond has been given to South, West and North, a club to East. Again there is a squeeze card and the necessary menaces, but the scheme blows up because West is not embarrassed by the lead of ♣ A. The position is not tight. It will be found in practice that the majority of squeezes occur when the declarer is in a position to win *all the remaining tricks but one*. Here he has only two winners and there are four cards left. The single word to describe this critical element in squeeze play is TIMING.

Right, now you understand what we mean when we talk about:

    MENACE CARDS
    SQUEEZE CARDS
    ENTRY CARDS
    TIMING

Study the diagrams that follow and in each case address your mind to the following questions in turn:

1 Is the TIMING right? This means, you must count the winners and note whether you are able to win 'all the remaining tricks but one'.
2 Is the MENACE situation satisfactory? This means, have you a two-card and a one-card menace both lying against the same opponent?
3 Is the ENTRY position satisfactory? This means, can you reach the weapons you propose to employ?
4 Is there a SQUEEZE CARD? You must be able to lead a card to which the opponent controlling two menaces is unable to follow.

Apply these tests to the following diagram:

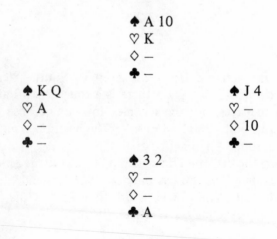

Timing? Right, you can win two of the last three tricks with top cards.

Entries? Right, you have communication with the dummy.

Squeeze card? Right, West, the player whom you hope to squeeze, cannot follow to the Ace of clubs.

Menaces? Wrong! you have only 1½ menaces lying against West, not two. When the Ace of clubs is led, West can discard a spade, since East also guards this suit.

Because the menace position is unsatisfactory, the squeeze will not work. But make East's spades 9 4 instead of J 4 and all is perfect.

Next case:

```
                    ♠ A J
                    ♡ —
                    ◇ —
                    ♣ A
   ♠ K Q                              ♠ 10 4
   ♡ A                                ♡ —
   ◇ —                                ◇ 10
   ♣ —                                ♣ —
                    ♠ 2
                    ♡ K
                    ◇ —
                    ♣ K
```

Here the timing is right – you have two tricks on top out of three. The menaces are right – West is threatened in both spades and hearts, with East out of the game. There is a squeeze card in clubs. But the entry situation is not right. When you lead the King of clubs West will throw the Ace of hearts; now your King of hearts will be a winner – but you cannot reach it. The squeeze works if you give North a low club instead of the Ace, so that South remains on lead after the play of the squeeze card. For the present you may accept this as a basic principle: *the squeeze card must be in the hand opposite the two-card menace.* Here the Ace of clubs was the squeeze card and it was in the same hand as ♠ A J.

You may wonder why we are looking at endings where the squeeze will not work. One reason is that, as we go along, you will become familiar with the basic conditions for a squeeze and will realize their importance. The other reason is that it is often possible to remedy the deficiencies by taking special measures. A large part of this book will be concerned with stratagems to that end.

Here is one more example of an ending where no squeeze is possible:

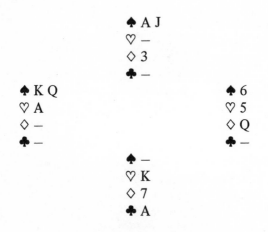

The timing is right, you have a squeeze card in clubs, West has controlling cards in two suits. What is wrong? You have no entry to dummy's spade menace, so when you lead your squeeze card, the Ace of clubs, West can cheerfully throw a spade.

In the remaining examples in this chapter the squeeze *will* work, but you have to play your cards in the right order. Remember, the squeeze card must come from the hand opposite the two-card menace.

```
              ♠ A J
              ♥ K
              ♦ A
              ♣ 2
 ♠ K Q                    ♠ —
 ♥ A                      ♥ —
 ♦ 2                      ♦ 10 9 8
 ♣ 3                      ♣ 6 5
              ♠ 3 2
              ♥ —
              ♦ 5
              ♣ Q J
```

The timing is right – there are five cards left and you have four top winners. West has exclusive control of two suits, spades and hearts. Either a diamond or a club must be the squeeze card. Which? It must be a club, from the hand opposite the two-card menace in spades. The diamond Ace must be played off early, since otherwise, when the squeeze card is led, West will not be under pressure. You must begin with a diamond to the Ace; then back to hand with a club and the second club will defeat West.

```
              ♠ 2
              ♥ A J
              ♦ —
              ♣ K J
 ♠ K Q                    ♠ 4 3
 ♥ K Q                    ♥ 4 3
 ♦ —                      ♦ A
 ♣ 2                      ♣ —
              ♠ A J
              ♥ —
              ♦ 2
              ♣ A Q
```

Again, the timing is right: you can take four out of the five remaining tricks with quick winners. West controls both spades and hearts, and there is a squeeze card in clubs. But do you play Queen of clubs to the King and back to the Ace, or the other way round? Apparently you have a two-card menace in spades and a two-card menace in hearts, but look again: there is no entry to ♡ A J, so you must treat spades as your two-card menace. The sequence is Ace of clubs followed by Queen to King, squeezing West. (Yes, if you want to be clever you can do it in a slightly different way: overtake ♣ Q with ♣ K, lead ♡ A, discarding ♣ A, and then the Jack of clubs is the squeeze card.)

               ♠ A J
               ♡ K
               ◇ 2
               ♣ —

♠ K Q   ♠ —
♡ A 4   ♡ —
◇ —   ◇ K Q J 10
♣ —   ♣ —

               ♠ 3 2
               ♡ —
               ◇ A 3
               ♣ —

For the sake of completeness, we show here a position where the timing needs correction. There are four cards left and you have only two top winners. Remember that you want to be in a position where you can win all the remaining tricks but one. If you play off your squeeze card, the Ace of diamonds, you will achieve nothing, because West has an idle card, his low heart. As the cards lie, you can develop an extra trick by beginning with a *low* diamond. East wins and must return a diamond, embarrassing his partner. This is a more advanced concept, known as 'rectifying the count'. We shall be saying much more about it in later chapters.

You may be thinking: 'Yes, I understand these terms – menaces, entry, timing, squeeze card – and I understand their importance. But how does that help me to play a full deal of 52 cards and develop the extra trick with a squeeze?' It is quite simple. In the next chapter we hide the squeeze pearl in the oyster of a full deal. You will find it easy to identify the various elements and foresee the ending.

2. The Simple Squeeze

When you look at two hands in combination, what should make you think that a squeeze may be possible?

Broadly speaking, you must be close to your contract in top tricks and you must have at least two potential tricks (menaces) that have not been included in your original tally. Almost *any* losing card has some menace potentiality, though of course some menaces are more menacing than others. With A x opposite Q x you have a guaranteed menace against a single opponent. Similarly, with K x opposite A Q x x you have a sure menace against one opponent, because it is impossible for both opponents to guard this suit. But we will find later that in some circumstances so benign a holding as x opposite A x may be the pivotal suit in a squeeze involving both opponents.

This chapter contains several examples of simple squeezes that can be foreseen at trick 1. Make a conscious effort, always, to identify the requirements we studied in the first chapter. Remember:

1 You must have two menace cards lying against the same opponent.
2 You must have an entry to whichever menace he unguards.
3 You must have a squeeze card to which he cannot follow suit.
4 The timing must be right – you must be stripped for action.

In each case study the initial diagram and identify the ending before you proceed to the analysis.

```
                        ♠ 9 2
                        ♡ A J 4
                        ◇ A Q J 7 5
                        ♣ K J 8
Contract: 7 NT            Deal A
Lead:        ♠ K
                        ♠ A J 4
                        ♡ 9 7 6
                        ◇ K 3
                        ♣ A Q 10 7 4
```

You are playing a 15–17 notrump, but in view of your useful club suit you open 1 NT, owing a point. Your partner, mindful of the Grand Slam prize (for the first Grand Slam bid and made during the evening), pays some passing attention to the presence of all the Aces, then carries you to 7 NT. West leads ♠ K. How will you carry off the prize?

First, *timing*.	Satisfactory in the sense that, barring a horrible break in diamonds, you have twelve tricks on top. You are able to win 'all the remaining tricks but one', the most favourable situation.
Second, *menaces*.	Not very promising, but they do exist. There is not (for present purposes) a menace card in diamonds, because you are assuming that the suit will be worth five tricks. The Jack of spades is clearly a menace card against West's Queen. The only other possibility lies in hearts. You will need to find West with ♡ K Q in addition to ♠ K Q. Well, he did look a bit smug when you contracted for 7 NT.
Third, *entries*.	The Jack of spades is a *one-card menace* and the hearts must be the *two-card menace*. So long as we retain ♡ A J intact and a low heart in our own hand there will be satisfactory communication.

11

Fourth, *squeeze card.* Either the fifth diamond or the fifth club would theoretically fill the bill; but the squeeze card must be held in the hand opposite the two-card menace, remember, so this function will be performed by a club.

So now you can construct the ending. You place West with what the French call the *mariage* in both majors and imagine the last three cards to be:

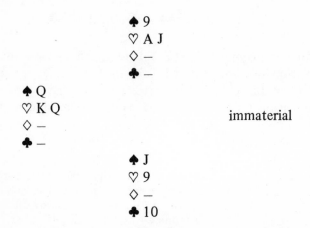

```
                    ♠ 9
                    ♡ A J
                    ◇ —
                    ♣ —
        ♠ Q
        ♡ K Q                   immaterial
        ◇ —
        ♣ —
                    ♠ J
                    ♡ 9
                    ◇ —
                    ♣ 10
```

When the last club is led West has to make a fatal discard. This was the full deal:

```
                    ♠ 9 2
                    ♡ A J 4
                    ◇ A Q J 7 5
                    ♣ K J 8
    ♠ K Q 10 5                      ♠ 8 7 6 3
    ♡ K Q 10 3                      ♡ 8 5 2
    ◇ 9 4           Deal A          ◇ 10 8 6 2
    ♣ 6 5 2                         ♣ 9 3
                    ♠ A J 4
                    ♡ 9 7 6
                    ◇ K 3
                    ♣ A Q 10 7 4
```

You will note that West might equally have led the King of hearts instead of the King of spades. What difference would that make? Correct, your two-card menace is now the A J of spades, so the squeeze card must come from North. You run the clubs first, then the diamonds, arriving at this position:

```
                    ♠ 9
                    ♡ J
                    ◇ 7
                    ♣ —
♠ K Q
♡ Q
◇ —                                     immaterial
♣ —
                    ♠ A J
                    ♡ 9
                    ◇ —
                    ♣ —
```

South discards a heart on the 7 of diamonds and West is squeezed.

Note that in this ending (and also the previous one) the one-card menace (♡ J) was in the same hand as the squeeze card. As a result, the squeeze was possible even though West was last to play. In technical terms, it was an automatic as opposed to a one-way squeeze. We say more about this distinction later in the chapter.

Now try this deal:

```
                    ♠ A 10 6 4
                    ♡ Q 8 5
                    ◇ K 6 5 2
                    ♣ 7 3
Contract: 6◇        Deal B
Lead:    ♡K
                    ♠ K 7 2
                    ♡ 9
                    ◇ A Q J 10 7 3
                    ♣ A K 4
```

13

You reach Six Diamonds and West leads the King of hearts. After examining his partner's card (which will signify an odd or even number in the suit), he switches to a trump.

You are going to ruff the third round of clubs, so you are in a position to make 'all the remaining tricks but one'. Unless you are particularly fortunate, you must expect a loser in spades. Your thoughts turn to a squeeze.

The timing, as we have already noted, is perfect. Menaces? No doubt West has the Ace of hearts, so the Queen of hearts is a one-card menace against him. So? Correct, you must find West in control of spades as well. Any combination including the Q J will do, and so will *any* four spades, because then again only West will be able to control the third round. Entries? No problem, you have good communication in spades. Squeeze card? The last diamond obviously.

The full deal turns out to be:

```
                    ♠ A 10 6 4
                    ♡ Q 8 5
                    ◇ K 6 5 2
                    ♣ 7 3
  ♠ J 8 5 3                        ♠ Q 9
  ♡ A K 10 3        Deal B         ♡ J 7 6 4 2
  ◇ 9 4                            ◇ 8
  ♣ J 8 5                          ♣ Q 10 9 6 2
                    ♠ K 7 2
                    ♡ 9
                    ◇ A Q J 10 7 3
                    ♣ A K 4
```

We have no doubt that you can visualize the three-card ending without the aid of a diagram. When the last diamond is led, North will hold ♠ A 10 and ♡ Q, West will be down to ♠ J 8 and ♡ A, and West will be discarding in front of dummy.

Another, quite easy, hand follows, so similar to the last one in all important elements that you may well visualize the ending immediately. But don't be too hasty, because you may have overlooked something.

♠ A 5
♡ A K 6 2
◇ Q 10 4 3
♣ K 9 3

Contract: 6 NT
Lead: ♠ K   Deal C

♠ J 8 4 3
♡ Q 5
◇ A K J 2
♣ A Q J

When West leads the King of spades and the dummy goes down, you think, 'Damn it, Six Diamonds would have been better. Annoying duplication in clubs. Now, what can I do in 6 NT? Well, there's a chance: West is marked with the Queen of spades. If he has the heart length as well . . .'

Yes, there would be a squeeze in that case . . . but have you considered the timing?

You have eleven top tricks and you need to make twelve, but you haven't lost a trick, so you are not in the ideal position of being able to make all the remaining tricks but one. Suppose you overlook this. You win with ♠ A and run off winners, arriving at this end position:

♠ 5
♡ A K 6
◇ 3
♣ —

♠ Q 10
♡ J 9 x
◇ —
♣ —   immaterial

♠ J 8 4
♡ 5
◇ J
♣ —

You lead the Jack of diamonds, but West is not embarrassed. He throws a spade and makes two more tricks.

Now look at the full deal:

```
                        ♠ A 5
                        ♡ A K 6 2
                        ◇ Q 10 4 3
                        ♣ K 9 3
  ♠ K Q 10 9 2                        ♠ 7 6
  ♡ J 9 7 4                           ♡ 10 8 3
  ◇ 9 5            Deal C             ◇ 8 7 6
  ♣ 10 7                              ♣ 8 6 5 4 2
                        ♠ J 8 4 3
                        ♡ Q 5
                        ◇ A K J 2
                        ♣ A Q J
```

The cards lay as you wanted, West having control of both majors. All goes well here if you improve the timing. It is quite easy to do that: you simply duck the first trick. Sometimes it is quite difficult to find a good way to improve the timing, and a later chapter deals exclusively with this problem.

Now, in case we are addressing a reader who is more experienced in squeeze play than we have so far assumed, we will concede that the slam *is* makable even if the Ace of spades is played at trick one. There is an animal known as the 'squeeze-without-the-count'. You will meet this deal again when we study positions where the timing is not satisfactory for a straightforward squeeze.

In the examples so far you have always known which opponent was going to be squeezed because one player was marked with control of one of the menaces. Often you don't know, when you begin, whether you will be squeezing West or East.

```
                    ♠ A K 7 3
                    ♡ A 7 5
                    ◇ Q 9 3
                    ♣ K 8 2

Contract: 6 NT     Deal D
Lead:      ♣ J

                    ♠ Q 6 2
                    ♡ K 6 4 2
                    ◇ A K 8
                    ♣ A Q 5
```

West leads a club against your contract of 6 NT. You have eleven tricks on top in Aces and Kings and two obvious chances for a twelfth: a 3–3 break in either spades or hearts, and you can test these suits in turn, because of course your first move will be to duck a round of hearts. But there is one additional chance: the same opponent may hold four hearts and four spades. The natural line of play is to win the club and duck a heart. Whatever the opponents return, you will play off the top cards in both minors, and also Ace and King of hearts, Ace and Queen of spades. Your last three cards will be:

```
                    ♠ K 7
                    ♡ —
                    ◇ —
                    ♣ 2


                    ♠ 6
                    ♡ 6
                    ◇ —
                    ♣ Q
```

You play off the Queen of clubs and make the contract if either major suit breaks and if either opponent holds the length in both majors.

You may say, such a hand plays itself. So it does, though if you knew nothing about squeeze play you might play the cards in the wrong order. The squeeze is said to be AUTO-MATIC. The features of an automatic squeeze are that the one-card menace is in the same hand as the squeeze card, and this means that the squeeze will work equally well against either opponent.

Now let's make a change in the diagram, placing the two menace cards in the *same* hand:

♠ A K 7 3
♥ A Q 7 5
◇ 5 4
♣ K 8 2

Contract: 6 NT
Lead: ◇ Q

Deal E

♠ Q 6 2
♥ K 6 4
◇ A 7 3
♣ A Q J 5

Again you are in 6 NT, and your chances are superficially the same as before. A 3–3 break in either major will provide you with a twelfth trick and perhaps you will be able to embarrass an opponent who holds length in both spades and hearts. Obviously you will duck the first round of diamonds, so that you will be in a position to win all the remaining tricks but one.

However, there is a difference: this time you may be able to squeeze West but you will never be able to squeeze East (unless, by chance, East has six diamonds, so that your third diamond will be an active menace).

The reason why you can forget about any possibility of squeezing East is that your two menaces in the major suits both lie under him: at the critical moment North will have to discard before East. Apart from a few rare situations where the same defender has to guard three suits, two menaces on the 'wrong' side of an opponent are useless. It is worth understanding points like this, because you will find it easier to make certain assumptions.

In the present case you will have a one-way squeeze against West if the deal is something like this:

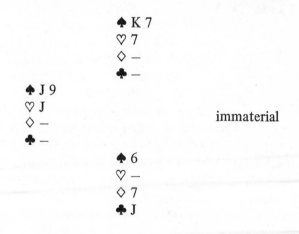

♠ A K 7 3
♡ A Q 7 5
◇ 5 4
♣ K 8 2

♠ J 9 5 4
♡ J 10 3 2
◇ Q J 9
♣ 10 3

Deal E

♠ 10 8
♡ 9 8
◇ K 10 8 6 2
♣ 9 7 6 4

♠ Q 6 2
♡ K 6 4
◇ A 7 3
♣ A Q J 5

You win the second round of diamonds and play three rounds of clubs, West discarding a diamond. It would be a mistake to play a fourth round of clubs at this point. Why? Because you would not be sure what to discard from dummy – you might throw a winner. First, therefore, you cash three rounds of one of the majors. You arrive at this end position:

♠ K 7
♡ 7
◇ –
♣ –

♠ J 9
♡ J
◇ –
♣ –

immaterial

♠ 6
♡ –
◇ 7
♣ J

The Jack of clubs squeezes West because he has to play in front of the dummy.

It is time now to look at a form of menace that is useful only in a one-way squeeze. This is the DIVIDED menace, where the components of a two-card menace lie partly in one hand, partly in the other. Instead of holding A J opposite x, for example, you hold J x opposite A x. These are common examples of a divided menace:

1.	A x		2.	A K x		3.	A x	
K x	— =		Q J x	— =		K Q	—
	Q x			10 x x			J x	

Assume in each case that you have a squeeze card to lead, and an additional menace against West on the table. This type of squeeze, as we have said, operates only against the opponent who is under the two-card menace. Here is an example:

```
              ♠ A K 5
              ♡ Q 6 3
              ◇ A K Q
              ♣ A K J 10
Contract: 7 NT   Deal F
Lead:      ♠ J
              ♠ Q 8 3
              ♡ A J 5
              ◇ 10 7 5 4 2
              ♣ Q 6
```

North opens Two Clubs and South responds 2 NT. Expecting his partner to hold ♡ A K, North advances to 7 NT.

A spade is led and South notes that if the diamonds break he will have thirteen top tricks. Unlucky, West shows out on the second round. Thirteen tricks have become eleven. A winning finesse of ♡ J will produce twelve. Perhaps East has a doubleton King of hearts? Not necessary, for if East has ♡ K in addition to ◇ J x x x you can be sure of the contract. You project the play to this three-card ending:

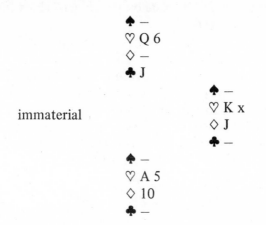

```
              ♠ —
              ♡ Q 6
              ◇ —
              ♣ J
                            ♠ —
                            ♡ K x
immaterial                  ◇ J
                            ♣ —

              ♠ —
              ♡ A 5
              ◇ 10
              ♣ —
```

The squeeze card, the Jack of clubs, must come from the hand opposite the two-card menace, as always. A divided menace, such as exists in hearts, is very common. On this deal you reach game in a minor suit after an opponent has opened the bidding:

```
              ♠ A 7 5
              ♡ 8 6 5 2
              ◇ K 9 4
              ♣ K 3 2

Contract: 5 ◇    Deal G
Lead:     ♡ K

              ♠ Q 8 3
              ♡ 9 7
              ◇ A Q J 10 6 5
              ♣ A J
```

West opens One Heart on your left and after two passes you bid Two Diamonds, with something in hand. Partner shows signs of life and you finish in Five Diamonds. West leads ♡ K and follows with ♡ A, East dropping the Queen, and ♡ J. East discards and you ruff.

21

Prospects may not seem too good, but if you can find East with the Queen of clubs you can be sure of the contract. Your aim is to discard a spade on the King of clubs and then exert pressure on West.

You must be careful not to waste entries to the table. You begin with a diamond to the 9. Then you finesse ♣ J – successfully. You cash the Ace, cross to ◇ K, and discard a spade on ♣ K. Because of your careful management you still have a trump in dummy, so you can return to hand without ruffing your menace in hearts. Now you run down the rest of the trumps, squeezing West at the finish. The full deal was:

```
                    ♠ A 7 5
                    ♡ 8 6 5 2
                    ◇ K 9 4
                    ♣ K 3 2
   ♠ K J 10                        ♠ 9 6 4 2
   ♡ A K J 10 3                    ♡ Q 4
   ◇ 7            Deal G           ◇ 8 3 2
   ♣ 10 8 5 4                      ♣ Q 9 7 6
                    ♠ Q 8 3
                    ♡ 9 7
                    ◇ A Q J 10 6 5
                    ♣ A J
```

You see that, after you have finessed ♣ J and discarded a spade on the King of clubs, you squeeze West, who must come down to ♠ K J and ♡ 10 in front of dummy's ♠ A 7 and ♡ 8?

You may have noted that the defence was not brilliant. Consider West's position after ♡ K has held the first trick. Partner's 4 is either a singleton (unlikely) or from Q 4 or Q 9 4. In any case it cannot cost to follow with ♡ J (you cannot be giving a trick to the Queen, because with 9 4 East would have begun an echo). As the cards lie, East wins the second trick and switches to a spade, destroying the entry for a squeeze.

One more general point is worth noting: when playing a simple squeeze *you never need more than one entry in the hand opposite the squeeze card*. Bearing this in mind, always play off as many top cards as you can before reaching the squeeze ending. Nothing is more annoying than to squeeze an opponent successfully and then not know which of your menace cards has been promoted. The declarer fell into this trap on the following deal:

```
                    ♠ A K 8
                    ♡ Q 9 7 3
                    ◇ A 7 5
                    ♣ K Q 3
  ♠ Q 10 9 7 4 2              ♠ 6 5
  ♡ A                         ♡ 8 2
  ◇ K 9 4        Deal H       ◇ J 10 6 3 2
  ♣ 10 8 5                    ♣ 9 7 6 4
                    ♠ J 3
                    ♡ K J 10 6 5 4
                    ◇ Q 8
                    ♣ A J 2
```

South opened One Heart, West overcalled with One Spade, and South finished in Six Hearts. Partly because a singleton Ace of trumps tends to be a liability (exposing the holder to a throw-in) and partly because he had no good alternative, West opened ♡ A. At trick two he switched to a club.

Remembering West's overcall, South saw good prospects of a squeeze in spades and diamonds. He played off a number of hearts and clubs, arriving at this position:

```
              ♠ A K 8
              ♡ —
              ◇ A 7 5
              ♣ —
♠ Q 10 9 7
♡ —
◇ K 9                    immaterial
♣ —
              ♠ J 3
              ♡ 10 6
              ◇ Q 8
              ♣ —
```

West was keeping count of the trumps, and when South led ♡ 10 he knew he still had to make two discards. He also knew (because he had a general count through his partner's discards) that he was going to be squeezed in spades and diamonds, unless his partner held ◇ Q. He therefore discarded ◇ 9 on this trick and ♠ 9 on the next trick. At this point South decided that West had unguarded the spades and threw another diamond from dummy, so he lost a spade at the finish.

The declarer could have avoided this folly by simply remembering the general rule that you need only one top card in the hand opposite the squeeze card. Here he must play off the Ace of diamonds before running off his winners.* To play off the Ace and King of spades is also good enough as the cards lie.

The rule to remember is this: If possible, reduce one of the menaces to a single card before playing the squeeze card. You will know whether this card has become a winner or not. If it is still a loser then the extra winner must come from the other menace suit and your choice of discard at the critical moment will not present a problem.

---

*This play of the Ace of diamonds bears a superficial resemblance to the *Vienna Coup* (see Chapter 4), but in a true *Vienna Coup* the play is made for a different reason.

Let us just review some of the general lessons that have been brought out in this chapter. There is a reference in each case to the deal that illustrated the principle.

The squeeze card must come from the hand opposite the two-card menace – Deal A.

An opponent may control a suit not just because he has honour cards but because he has length – Deal B.

Aim to bring about a situation where you can win all the remaining tricks but one – Deal C.

When the one-card menace is in the same hand as the squeeze card the squeeze is automatic and will work equally well against either opponent – Deal D.

When the two menaces are in the same hand the squeeze can succeed only against the player who plays in front of the menaces – Deal E.

When the two-card menace is 'divided', the one-card menace must be in the same hand as the top entry and only the player in front of these menaces can be squeezed – Deal F.

You may need to take care with entries so as not to imperil any of your menace cards – Deal G.

Strip the hand as far as you can before playing the squeeze card, to avoid any guessing at the finish. One top entry is all you need opposite the squeeze card – Deal H (also Deal E).

3. Arranging the Menaces

In the examples we have been looking at so far there has been little or no work to do in setting up the squeeze. But life is not always so kind. One or more of the conditions necessary for the squeeze may not be present at the outset. The next three chapters are concerned with overcoming slight problems that may exist in connection with menaces, entries or timing. First, we consider menaces.

As we have already observed, a single menace that is controlled by both opponents is of value in only one rare type of squeeze. Very often, a simple manoeuvre will place the control of a menace card in the hand of just one opponent. The process is known as 'isolating the menace'.

Isolating a menace by ruffing

Observe the heart situation in the deal below – K x opposite A x x x. Initially the suit may be divided 4–3, allowing both opponents to control the third round. But if you ruff the third round, then only one opponent will be able to control the fourth card, and you hope this will be the right opponent for your general plan.

```
                    ♠ A Q 6
                    ♡ A 7 4 3
                    ◇ K 5 2
                    ♣ 6 4 3
        ♠ K 10 4                    ♠ 9 8 5 2
        ♡ Q 10 8 6                  ♡ J 9 2
        ◇ 6                         ◇ 10 9 8
        ♣ A K J 9 5                 ♣ Q 10 7
                    ♠ J 7 3
                    ♡ K 5
                    ◇ A Q J 7 4 3
                    ♣ 8 2
```

Sitting South, you play in Five Diamonds after West has opened the bidding with One Club. West leads ♣ K and you ruff the third round.

You have ten tricks on top, assuming that the spade finesse is right. A doubleton King of spades would give you the extra trick, but you have an additional chance: if West has the King of spades and four hearts, he can be squeezed.

After drawing trumps and finessing ♠ Q successfully, you play three rounds of hearts, ruffing in hand. The end position is:

```
                      ♠ A 6
                      ♡ 7
                      ◇ —
                      ♣ —
   ♠ K 10
   ♡ Q                             immaterial
   ◇ —
   ♣ —
                      ♠ J 7
                      ♡ —
                      ◇ 4
                      ♣ —
```

When you lead the 4 of diamonds, West is squeezed. Note that we can mark the East hand as 'immaterial' precisely because his three hearts have been extracted. If this had not been done, East would have been able to control the third round of hearts and West would have been off the hook.

Sometimes you have to work a little harder to isolate the menace.

                    ♠ 10 9
                    ♡ A Q 5
                    ◇ 9 7 6 5 3 2
                    ♣ 6 3
♠ 5 4   ♠ 8 7 6
♡ K J 9 6 4   ♡ 10 8
◇ A Q J 4   ◇ K 10 8
♣ Q 8   ♣ 10 9 7 5 2
                    ♠ A K Q J 3 2
                    ♡ 7 3 2
                    ◇ —
                    ♣ A K J 4

After West has opened One Heart you discover that your partner has a heart control and bid boldly to Six Spades. West opens ♠ 5 – a shrewd stroke, as it happens, because it prevents you from ruffing two clubs.

You can see six spades in your own hand, at least three clubs, and two hearts. How are you going to play the clubs? A successful finesse would win the contract unless West ruffed the second round, but you should take note of the fact that West has not led a high diamond, as he surely would have done from A K. If East has Ace or King of diamonds, West is likely to hold the Queen of clubs. Thus your best chance to arrive at four tricks in clubs is to play off the top clubs and ruff the third round, playing West for Q x x.

While thinking about the clubs, don't forget that there are squeeze possibilities in the red suits. If West has five hearts, as is likely, and four diamonds, then he can be squeezed, provided that East's diamonds have been extracted. Therefore the first, cost-nothing, move after you have won the opening lead in dummy is to ruff a diamond.

You then play off Ace and King of clubs, as planned. West's Queen appears, which does you no harm. You ruff ♣ 4, ruff another diamond, and draw trumps. After a finesse of ♡ Q and another diamond ruff you arrive at this end position:

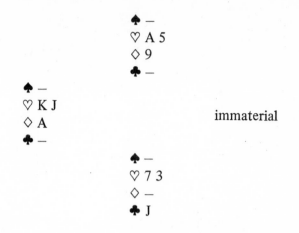

```
            ♠ —
            ♡ A 5
            ◇ 9
            ♣ —
♠ —
♡ K J
◇ A                      immaterial
♣ —
            ♠ —
            ♡ 7 3
            ◇ —
            ♣ J
```

Again we can mark East as 'immaterial' or 'innocuous', because his three diamonds have been expunged. You lead ♠ 3 and make an overtrick. That is how pairs tournaments are won!

Isolating a menace by ducking

Ruffing the early rounds of a suit is not the only way to isolate a menace. Often this can be done by the simplest form of ducking play. Suppose that a suit is divided in this way:

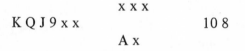

```
                  x x x
K Q J 9 x x                      10 8
                  A x
```

West, who is marked with length, leads the King. If South wins, the suit will be useless for squeeze purposes. By ducking, declarer leaves West in sole control. This form of play often goes hand in hand with improvement of the timing, as in this example:

                    ♠ A K 7 4
                    ♡ 5 2
                    ◇ K 7 5 3
                    ♣ K J 6

Contract: 6 NT
Lead: ♡ Q

                    ♠ 8 5
                    ♡ A K 9
                    ◇ A Q 4 2
                    ♣ A Q 7 3

South plays in 6 NT after West has opened with a pre-emptive Three Hearts. West leads ♡ Q and East follows suit with the 6.

There are eleven tricks in Aces and Kings, twelve if the diamonds are 3–2. Declarer should assume, therefore, that diamonds are 4–1 and should consider where that leaves him. Obviously, since the hand contains no tenaces, the twelfth trick (assuming the diamonds to be recalcitrant) must come from a squeeze.

To improve the timing, South must aim to lose an early trick. In which suit? If he ducks a diamond or a heart he sacrifices one of his own potential menace cards. The cure for one disease (timing) is ineffective if the patient merely contracts another (insufficiency of menace cards). No, the trick must be surrendered in spades. There is another advantage in this: after a round of spades has been ducked, only one opponent will be able to control the suit.

So the first move is to win with ♡ K and duck a round of spades. Now, bearing in mind that West is marked with at least six, probably seven hearts, the contract can hardly fail.

Suppose, first, that when they take the spade trick the defenders play a heart or a diamond. South tests the diamonds by playing off Ace and Queen. Now, if West has the long diamonds he can be squeezed in diamonds and hearts; if East has the long diamonds declarer will approach this ending:

♠ A K 7
♡ —
◇ —
♣ —

♠ 5
♡ 9
◇ 4
♣ —

At this point West has the master heart, East the master diamond, so neither will be able to guard the spades.

It would be somewhat better play by the defenders to return a spade after taking the first trick in this suit. By so doing, they break the communications in one suit at least. Suppose that this is the full hand:

♠ A K 7 4
♡ 5 2
◇ K 7 5 3
♣ K J 6

♠ Q 9 3
♡ Q J 10 8 7 4 3
◇ 6
♣ 9 5

♠ J 10 6 2
♡ 6
◇ J 10 9 8
♣ 10 8 4 2

♠ 8 5
♡ A K 9
◇ A Q 4 2
♣ A Q 7 3

Playing in 6 NT, you win the heart lead and duck a spade. The defenders return a spade. At this point it would be incorrect to test the diamonds by playing off two rounds. Best is to lead a third spade and two rounds of clubs. You learn then that there is no room in the West hand for four diamonds, so you plan a spade-diamond squeeze against East. You run the four clubs and ♡ A, then cross to ◇ K, and by this time East will be under the hammer.

The squeeze card in this sequence of play is the Ace of hearts, and it may have struck you that on this occasion the squeeze card was in the same hand as the two-card menace, contrary to the principle stated in the last chapter. This is possible because in diamonds there is a double menace, K x in one hand, Q x x in the other. This allows for more flexibility in the position of the menaces.

That declarer should duck a round of spades on the last hand was fairly obvious. A similar type of play is needed on the next deal, but few players would spot it without the assistance given by the bidding:

♠ 6 5 3
♡ A K 5 2
◇ 8 7 4
♣ K 6 2

Contract: 4 ♠
Lead: ◇ K

♠ A K Q J 10
♡ 4
◇ 9 3
♣ A 9 7 4 3

West, playing the Roman system, opens Two Hearts. This signifies at least five hearts and at least four clubs. You reach Four Spades and the defence begins with ◇ A K and a third diamond, which you ruff. You play off two top trumps and on the second round West discards a heart. The position is now:

♠ 6
♡ A K 5 2
◇ —
♣ K 6 2

♠ Q J
♡ 4
◇ —
♣ A 9 7 4 3

As West has turned up with one spade and three diamonds you know his shape exactly: 1-5-3-4. If you draw the last two trumps you will put West under some pressure, but he can defeat you by discarding hearts, leaving his partner to control the third round of this suit.

This is frustrating, because you feel there ought to be a squeeze against West in hearts and clubs. So there is, but to bring it about you must both restore the timing and isolate the menace in hearts. You do this at one stroke by ducking the first or second round of hearts. Dummy's third trump is protection against a fourth round of diamonds. Say that East wins the second round of hearts and leads a club. You win with the Ace and play off two more trumps, squeezing West. The full hand is:

```
                    ♠ 6 5 3
                    ♡ A K 5 2
                    ◇ 8 7 4
                    ♣ K 6 2
  ♠ 8                              ♠ 9 7 4 2
  ♡ Q 10 9 7 6                     ♡ J 8 3
  ◇ A K 6                          ◇ Q J 10 5 2
  ♣ Q J 8 5                        ♣ 10
                    ♠ A K Q J 10
                    ♡ 4
                    ◇ 9 3
                    ♣ A 9 7 4 3
```

Note that it was essential to give up an *early* round of hearts: if you play off Ace, King and another, West will play a fourth round, both extinguishing the menace card and causing you to lose trump control.

One other idea may have occurred to you: why not discard a club on the third round of diamonds? Then, apparently, you can isolate the menace in hearts by ruffing the third round. On many rather similar hands this would be good play, but it doesn't quite work here because East can lead a fourth diamond, forcing you to ruff in front of West. Then you have to trump to spare for a ruff of the third round of hearts. West keeps clubs, East keeps hearts, and the contract is defeated.

Transferring the menace

There is another way of arranging the menaces to suit your purpose: instead of extracting the control held by one opponent, you transfer control from one opponent to the other. Suppose that a suit is distributed in this fashion:

```
                    A K 6
      Q 7 3                       10 8 5
                    J 9 4
```

Here you have a divided menace against West, but suppose that West has no other valuable goods. There may be a squeeze against East, but not against West, who has no other menace to protect. If you have reason to place West with the Queen you can lead the Jack, forcing West to cover and establishing the 9 as a menace against East's 10. This recherché play is known as 'transferring the menace'.

```
                    ♠ 8 5 3
                    ♡ K 6 4 2
                    ◇ A Q 6 5
                    ♣ A 4
    ♠ A K J 10 6                   ♠ 9 4
    ♡ 10 7 5                       ♡ 9
    ◇ 8                            ◇ J 10 9 4 3
    ♣ K 9 7 3                      ♣ J 8 6 5 2
                    ♠ Q 7 2
                    ♡ A Q J 8 3
                    ◇ K 7 2
                    ♣ Q 10
```

You play in Four Hearts after West has opened One Spade. East ruffs the third round of spades and switches to a diamond, which you win in dummy. On the first round of trumps East shows out, discarding a low club.

At the beginning of the play you expected to make the contract either by finding the diamonds 3-3 or by squeezing West, should he hold four diamonds and ♣ K. But now East has turned up with only three cards in the major suits, so assuredly it is East who will hold the long diamonds. West must hold the King of clubs for his opening bid, but perhaps East holds the Jack of clubs?

At an early stage you lead the Queen of clubs, forcing a cover from West. This transfers the menace to East and the last trump will squeeze East in clubs and diamonds. Your last three cards will be ♡ 8, ◇ 7 and ♣ 10; East will have to discard from ◇ 10 9 and ♣ J.

Look for the same idea in this deal:

```
                    ♠ 8 5 3
                    ♡ K J 9
                    ◇ Q 10 7 2
                    ♣ A 9 4
   ♠ Q 10 6                        ♠ A J 9 4
   ♡ 8 6 4 2                       ♡ 5
   ◇ A K 5 4                       ◇ J 8 6 3
   ♣ 8 2                           ♣ J 10 6 3
                    ♠ K 7 2
                    ♡ A Q 10 7 3
                    ◇ 9
                    ♣ K Q 7 5
```

You are in Four Hearts and West leads the ◇ K. East plays the 8 to show an even number and West perhaps takes this also to indicate strength in spades. At any rate, he switches to a low spade. East wins with the Ace and returns the 4, which you win. On the second round of trumps East shows out, discarding a spade.

You have a spade loser and need to look after the fourth round of clubs. All the indications are that if anyone has long clubs it will be East. At present you have no menace against him in either spades or diamonds, but perhaps you can transfer the diamond menace? You accomplish this by the neat stroke of leading ◇ Q from dummy and discarding your spade loser. West wins and leads ♠ Q, which you ruff. You arrive at this ending:

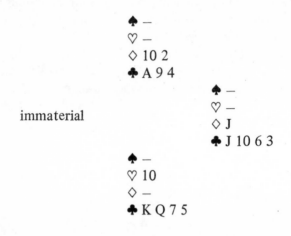

```
                    ♠ —
                    ♡ —
                    ◇ 10 2
                    ♣ A 9 4
                                   ♠ —
                                   ♡ —
       immaterial                  ◇ J
                                   ♣ J 10 6 3
                    ♠ —
                    ♡ 10
                    ◇ —
                    ♣ K Q 7 5
```

On the last heart you throw a diamond from dummy and East must succumb.

Retaining the right menaces

Sometimes it is not too clear which of your own cards you should retain as menaces. Most players would make the wrong discard at trick 4 on the following deal:

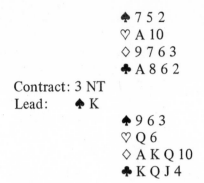

♠ 7 5 2
♡ A 10
◊ 9 7 6 3
♣ A 8 6 2

Contract: 3 NT
Lead:　　♠ K

♠ 9 6 3
♡ Q 6
◊ A K Q 10
♣ K Q J 4

You play in 3 NT after West has made an overcall of One Heart. West leads the King of spades and follows with Ace and another. East cashes a thirteenth spade. How do you discard from your own hand and from dummy?

A problem will arise only if West has J x x x of diamonds. If East has the four diamonds there will be a marked finesse, so you must be reluctant to throw ◊ 10. A club looks safe, but there is a drawback in this because you must expect the Ace of hearts to be forced out on the next lead. Then if clubs are 4–1 the suit will be blocked.

The card you can spare best is a heart. Presumably West has K J, so your ♡ Q is not a valuable card in any event. Remember that a one-card menace controlled by the player who sits over it is a dead letter unless there is compensation in the form of additional entries.

So you discard a heart from hand. West throws a heart and now you have to play from dummy. Be careful to throw a diamond, not a club. Remember, your only fear is that West may hold ◊ J x x x, and if that is the case you will want to squeeze him in hearts and diamonds. The squeeze card must come from dummy, and for this reason you must keep four clubs on the table.

This is the full hand:

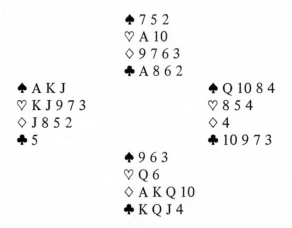

```
              ♠ 7 5 2
              ♡ A 10
              ◇ 9 7 6 3
              ♣ A 8 6 2
♠ A K J                        ♠ Q 10 8 4
♡ K J 9 7 3                    ♡ 8 5 4
◇ J 8 5 2                      ◇ 4
♣ 5                            ♣ 10 9 7 3
              ♠ 9 6 3
              ♡ Q 6
              ◇ A K Q 10
              ♣ K Q J 4
```

Against 3 NT, the defenders begin with four spade tricks. You must throw a heart from hand, a diamond from dummy. East switches to a heart, covered by the Queen, King and Ace. You play two rounds of diamonds and four rounds of clubs, finishing in dummy. Meanwhile, you squeeze West in hearts and diamonds. If you make any other discards on the fourth spade, you fail.

4.   Arranging the Entries

To bring off a squeeze, as with many enterprises in life, you need to be in the right place at the right time. This means, in particular, that at the moment when you play your squeeze card, forcing an opponent to unguard one of your menaces, you must be able to reach the menace card that has been established. Often a form of unblocking play is necessary. The classic example is the so-called *Vienna Coup*. This is the deal that puzzled café society in 1864:

```
                    ♠ A Q
                    ♡ 5
                    ◇ A Q 9 7 5 3
                    ♣ A K Q 3
   ♠ 9 8 7 6 5 4                    ♠ K 2
   ♡ 7 6                            ♡ 10 9 8 3 2
   ◇ K 2                            ◇ J 10 8
   ♣ J 5 4                          ♣ 10 8 2
                    ♠ J 10 3
                    ♡ A K Q J 4
                    ◇ 6 4
                    ♣ 9 7 6
```

A leading whist player of the time challenged his friends to make thirteen tricks with clubs as trumps and North on lead.

Most of those who accepted the challenge lost their money. A modern player would not find the play difficult. South has only eleven top tricks, counting the diamond finesse, but East has to guard three suits, and in such cases, as we shall see in a later chapter, it is often possible to develop two extra tricks. The problem here is one of entries. Suppose that the declarer (the term is an anachronism) begins by playing off four rounds of clubs. East is under the hammer, but he can survive for the moment by discarding a heart, conceding one trick only. Suppose that South then runs the hearts. He reaches this position:

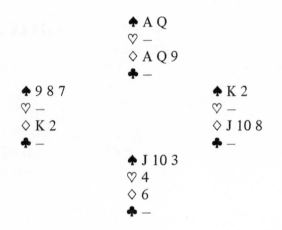

On the last heart dummy throws a spade and East is squeezed to the extent that he must unguard the King of spades. However, this does not profit the declarer because he is never able to enjoy his spade winners.

The simple solution is to cash the Ace of spades at an earlier stage. In technical terms, a *Vienna Coup* consists of the play of a high card in a menace suit (the Ace of spades) so that a one-card menace (the Jack of spades) will be correctly positioned for an automatic squeeze against the right-hand opponent. That may sound ponderous, but if you understand the definition you will not miss the play. And this is a useful tip: as mentioned in Chapter 2, only one entry is required in the hand opposite the squeeze card. Obviously you are not going to play off the top diamonds, so it must be right to cash the Ace of spades if you are planning a squeeze.

The next example would deceive some players because the unblocking play is made from the declarer's hand, not dummy's.

♠ K J 8 7 4
♡ 10 4 2
◊ K 10 6
♣ Q 5

Contract: 4 ♠
Lead: ◊ 8

♠ A Q 5 2
♡ A K 6
◊ J 9 5 3
♣ A 7

The defence against Four Spades begins with a diamond to the Queen, Ace of diamonds, West discarding a club, and a diamond ruff. West exits with a trump and shows out when you draw the last trump. These cards are left:

♠ J 8 7
♡ 10 4 2
◊ —
♣ Q 5

♠ Q 5
♡ A K 6
◊ J
♣ A 7

You could discard a club on the Jack of diamonds, but since you would be ruffing the second club in the long trump hand, this would not carry you much further. Your only hope (apart from the very slight chance of dropping a doubleton Q J of hearts) lies in a squeeze. Since West has turned up with a singleton diamond and only two trumps, there is a good chance of finding him with five hearts and the King of clubs. You foresee an ending in which dummy will have the Queen of clubs, a heart, and a trump (the squeeze card), while you will be down to ♡ K 6 and ♣ 7. To bring this about, you must discard a heart on ◊ J, cash ♣ A (the

Vienna Coup), then run the trumps. This wins when the full hand is:

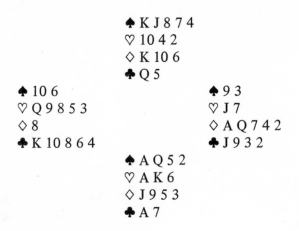

```
                    ♠ K J 8 7 4
                    ♡ 10 4 2
                    ◇ K 10 6
                    ♣ Q 5
  ♠ 10 6                            ♠ 9 3
  ♡ Q 9 8 5 3                       ♡ J 7
  ◇ 8                               ◇ A Q 7 4 2
  ♣ K 10 8 6 4                      ♣ J 9 3 2
                    ♠ A Q 5 2
                    ♡ A K 6
                    ◇ J 9 5 3
                    ♣ A 7
```

The sequence of play is three rounds of diamonds, two trumps, one top heart (at most), Jack of diamonds (discarding a heart from dummy), Ace of clubs, and all the trumps, squeezing West.

It is easy to recognize the possibility of a *Vienna Coup* when you have a holding such as A x opposite Q x, but just as often the coup is needed to establish a low card as a menace.

```
                    ♠ 8 4 2
                    ♡ A K 10 4
                    ◇ A Q 10 3
                    ♣ K 5
  ♠ A K Q 9 5 3                     ♠ 10 7 6
  ♡ Q 3                             ♡ J 9 6 2
  ◇ K 7                             ◇ J 8 6 4 2
  ♣ 10 3 2                          ♣ 9
                    ♠ J
                    ♡ 8 7 5
                    ◇ 9 5
                    ♣ A Q J 8 7 6 4
```

The bidding goes:

South	West	North	East
–	1♠	dble	No
3♣	No	3♠	No
5♣	No	6♣	No
No	No		

The defence begins with two rounds of spades. You ruff and draw two trumps, East discarding a diamond on the second round.

You can be fairly sure now that West began with nine cards in the black suits. Instead of a desperate finesse in one of the red suits, you should turn your mind to the possibility of a squeeze against East.

If you are going to squeeze East you must establish a one-card menace in your own hand. This must be in hearts. So the play is: draw trumps, discarding a heart or a diamond from the table, finesse ◊ Q, cash ♡ A K (*Vienna Coup*), ruff a spade, and play off the trumps, reaching this position:

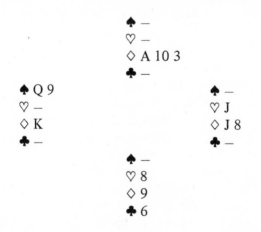

Now the 8 of hearts is your one-card menace and East has no good discard on the last club.

So much for the *Vienna Coup*, to which, perhaps, excessive importance has been attached in bridge literature. More often, the declarer's problem is simply to play side suits in the right order.

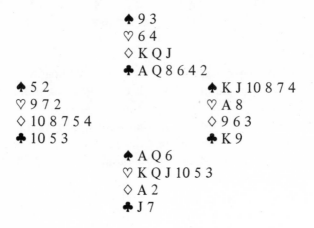

```
              ♠ 9 3
              ♡ 6 4
              ◇ K Q J
              ♣ A Q 8 6 4 2
♠ 5 2                        ♠ K J 10 8 7 4
♡ 9 7 2                      ♡ A 8
◇ 10 8 7 5 4                 ◇ 9 6 3
♣ 10 5 3                     ♣ K 9
              ♠ A Q 6
              ♡ K Q J 10 5 3
              ◇ A 2
              ♣ J 7
```

With both sides vulnerable the bidding goes:

South	West	North	East
1♡	No	2♣	2♠
4♡	No	5♡	No
6♡	No	No	No

West leads ♠ 5 and South wins the first trick with the Queen. In view of East's overcall at the Two level, South cannot expect to ruff the third round of spades in safety, so he leads the King of hearts, losing to the Ace. East returns a spade and the Ace holds.

Now the 6 of spades is a menace against East and, on the assumption that East holds the King of clubs, dummy's ♣ A Q represent a two-card menace. Since the eventual squeeze card will be a heart, South must play off the diamonds at an early stage. However, it would be a mistake to draw trumps, because then, after cashing the diamond winners, declarer would have no quick entry to hand. Despite the slight risk that the third round of diamonds may be ruffed, South must play three rounds of diamonds immediately, returning to hand with dummy's second trump. Then he has a simple squeeze against East in the black suits.

Note also, that if East holds up the Ace of hearts for one round declarer must cash the diamonds before leading another trump.

We noted in the last chapter that the presence of a double menace, such as K x in one hand, A x x in the other, will at times enable the declarer to overcome what would otherwise be an unsatisfactory placement of the menace cards. Such combinations therefore need to be preserved.

♠ 7 4 2
♡ 5 3
◇ A 6
♣ 8 7 6 4 3 2

Contract: 4 ♠
Lead: ♠ A

♠ K Q J 10 3
♡ A K 10
◇ K 10 5
♣ K 10

West, who has doubled your One Spade opening, begins with the Ace of trumps against Four Spades and follows with Ace of clubs and another club, which East ruffs. East exits with a second round of trumps and West discards a heart.

After this devilish defence you are in some difficulty. You cannot do anything with the clubs owing to shortage of entries, and there is only one trump in dummy to take care of your two losers in the red suits. However, you have a menace against West in clubs and West may have sole control of hearts or diamonds. What you should realize is that you cannot in any event squeeze West in hearts and clubs, because after ruffing the third round of diamonds you will have no entry to dummy, where the club menace lies. Therefore you must ruff a heart, not a diamond. You return to hand with a

club ruff and play off all the trumps, squeezing West if he
began with ◇ Q J x x. This is the full hand:

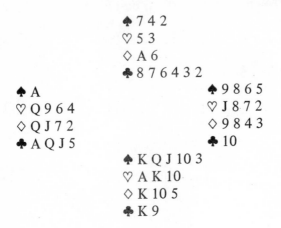

♠ 7 4 2
♡ 5 3
◇ A 6
♣ 8 7 6 4 3 2

♠ A
♡ Q 9 6 4
◇ Q J 7 2
♣ A Q J 5

♠ 9 8 6 5
♡ J 8 7 2
◇ 9 8 4 3
♣ 10

♠ K Q J 10 3
♡ A K 10
◇ K 10 5
♣ K 9

At the finish you hold ◇ A 6 and ♣ 8 in dummy, ◇ K 10 5
in your own hand. West, by this time, will have been forced
to unguard one suit or the other.

On this final deal you need to think clearly at trick 1:

♠ K 5
♡ A K Q
◇ K Q 9 6 4
♣ K J 4

Contract: 7 NT
Lead: ♠ 10

♠ A J 8 2
♡ 10 7 3
◇ A 8 5 2
♣ A 6

You open 1 NT as South and after routine inquiries your
partner lands you in 7 NT. West leads the 10 of spades. Plan
the play.

It is tempting in a way to let the first spade run to the
Jack, because if you can make five tricks in diamonds you
will then have thirteen tricks on top. However, you are in a

grand slam, so this is not the moment to play without looking round every corner.

West would hardly have led from Q 10 9 against a grand slam in notrumps, so you must consider whether there could be any advantage in going up with ♠ K, to improve your entry position. A problem will arise only if East has four diamonds; if West has ◊ J 10 x x you can pick them up by the standard safety play of beginning with a low diamond to the Ace.

If East has the four diamonds, you will have at best twelve tricks on top, assuming as you must that both Queen finesses are right. Your only chance of a thirteenth will be to find East with long spades in addition to long diamonds.

Do you begin to see now why it would be a mistake to let the first spade run to the Jack? You lay down the Ace of diamonds, finding that West is void. Now, because of lack of communication, there is nothing you can do even if the full hand is like this:

```
              ♠ K 5
              ♡ A K Q
              ◊ K Q 9 6 4
              ♣ K J 4
  ♠ 10 9 4                      ♠ Q 7 6 3
  ♡ J 8 6 4 2                   ♡ 9 5
  ◊ —                           ◊ J 10 7 3
  ♣ Q 10 8 3 2                  ♣ 9 7 5
              ♠ A J 8 2
              ♡ 10 7 3
              ◊ A 8 5 2
              ♣ A 6
```

If you go up with ♠ K at trick 1 the hand develops quite easily. When a diamond to the Ace reveals the break, you steel yourself to the club finesse and run off three hearts and three clubs. East must make a fatal discard on the third heart.

It is true that if you let the first spade run to the Jack you could still make the contract, but only if you gave up the chance of picking up four diamonds in the West hand. You could reach an end position in which South, on lead, held a diamond and a spade, North ◊ Q 9.

There is no doubt that on balance it is correct to go up with ♠ K at trick 1, retaining all chances. This form of play is often necessary, for entry reasons, even when there is no certainty that the subsequent finesse will succeed.

5.   Arranging the Timing

As we have noted on many occasions, an opponent can be squeezed only when all his idle cards have been played. You may recall this four-card ending from the first chapter:

```
                    ♠ A J
                    ♡ K
                    ◊ 4
                    ♣ —
    ♠ K Q                          ♠ —
    ♡ A                            ♡ —
    ◊ 6                            ◊ 10 9 8
    ♣ —                            ♣ 5
                    ♠ 2
                    ♡ —
                    ◊ 3 2
                    ♣ A
```

South has the lead at notrumps. There are two menace cards lying against West and a squeeze card, the Ace of clubs. But it is a squeeze card only in the sense that West cannot follow suit: it does not embarrass him because West has a spare card, the low diamond. If you remove a diamond from each hand, then the squeeze does gain a trick. This chapter is concerned with manoeuvres to bring about the desired situation where an opponent has no safe discard.

Very often the declarer has an opportunity to 'rectify the count', as it is called, on the opening lead:

                    ♠ 6 4
                    ♡ K Q 7 5 2
                    ◇ A Q 5
                    ♣ A 9 6

♠ K Q J 9 7 3 2   ♠ 5
♡ 8 4   ♡ 9 6 3
◇ 9 4   ◇ J 10 7 3
♣ 10 2   ♣ Q J 8 5 4

                    ♠ A 10 8
                    ♡ A J 10
                    ◇ K 8 6 2
                    ♣ K 7 3

South opens a strong notrump, West overcalls with Two
Spades, and North takes a pot shot at 6 NT. West leads the
King of spades.

South can count eleven tricks in top cards. A 3–3 break in
diamonds would produce a twelfth; failing that, it may be
possible to squeeze East in the minor suits, because obviously
West has six or seven spades.

If South captures the spade lead with the Ace he loses the
chance for a squeeze. He reaches this type of ending:

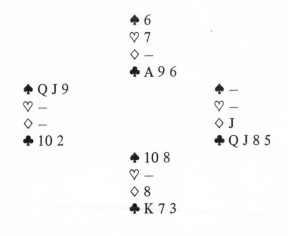

                    ♠ 6
                    ♡ 7
                    ◇ —
                    ♣ A 9 6

♠ Q J 9   ♠ —
♡ —   ♡ —
◇ —   ◇ J
♣ 10 2   ♣ Q J 8 5

                    ♠ 10 8
                    ♡ —
                    ◇ 8
                    ♣ K 7 3

The squeeze card, the ♡ 7, turns out to be a toothless wonder: East discards a club and South has no play for an extra trick. It should be plain that if South 'rectifies the count' by ducking at trick one, East cannot withstand the pressure.

Before giving more examples of this kind, we should perhaps correct a possible misapprehension. While it is normally the declarer's aim to bring about a situation in which he can win all the remaining tricks but one, this often cannot be conveniently done. However, it may well be possible for the squeeze to operate when a trick still has to be lost. We will see examples of this in the next chapter, under the heading 'Squeeze-without-the-count'.

To restore the timing in the example above was easy in the sense that a spade trick could be surrendered without any damage to entries or menaces. Sometimes it is not quite so clear which trick you should give up.

♠ A J 2
♡ Q 7 4
◇ K 8 3
♣ A 6 4 2

Contract: 6 ♡
Lead: ♠ K

♠ 5
♡ A K J 10 6
◇ A Q J 4
♣ Q 7 3

You play in Six Hearts after West has overcalled in spades. West leads the King of spades. You win with the Ace and examine your prospects.

You are one trick short. Presumably West has the King of clubs, so a lead towards the Queen is not likely to produce a trick. Ah, but if West has K Q of spades and King of clubs there should be a one-way squeeze. You envisage an ending in which West, with ♠ Q and ♣ K x, will be discarding in front of dummy's ♠ J and ♣ A 6. But when you look at this more closely you realize that the timing is wrong. When you have played off all the red suit winners you will have three clubs left and a dead position.

Perhaps you can rectify the count? But it's not so easy. If you duck a club East may win and return a club, knocking out the Ace. If you give up a spade, discarding a club instead of ruffing, West will play a third spade, extinguishing the one-card menace.

A throw-in, then? lead ♠ J at trick eleven, forcing a return from the King of clubs. No, that does not work either, because after you have played off your winners in the red suits (necessary to arrive at the three-card ending) you will have no entry to dummy.

In the end you may decide to play West for a doubleton King of clubs. You may be lucky, you may be told you have misplayed the hand.

Sorry, we caught you on the first trick. You must let the King of spades hold. Say that West exits safely in trumps. You play off all the trumps, Ace of spades, and all the diamonds, squeezing West if he began with ♠ K Q and ♣ K.

This is another deal where you have to be alive early on to the possibility of a squeeze:

```
              ♠ K 7 4 2
              ♡ Q 8 3
              ◇ K 9 4
              ♣ 9 5 3
♠ 6                        ♠ 9 3
♡ A K J 7 5 2              ♡ 10 4
◇ J 5                      ◇ Q 10 8 6 2
♣ 10 8 7 2                 ♣ K Q 6 4
              ♠ A Q J 10 8 5
              ♡ 9 6
              ◇ A 7 3
              ♣ A J
```

You play in Four Spades after West has overcalled in hearts. West leads ♡ K and must continue the suit to kill dummy's Queen. East ruffs the third round. If you overruff you cannot avoid the loss of a diamond and a club. Your only live chance is to find East with long diamonds and both club honours. To rectify the count you must discard a diamond on the third heart, instead of overruffing. East will probably exit with the King of clubs and you reach this ending:

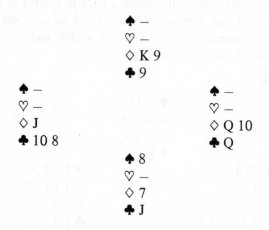

```
              ♠ —
              ♡ —
              ◇ K 9
              ♣ 9
♠ —                        ♠ —
♡ —                        ♡ —
◇ J                        ◇ Q 10
♣ 10 8                     ♣ Q
              ♠ 8
              ♡ —
              ◇ 7
              ♣ J
```

You lead the 8 of spades, discarding a club from dummy, and East has no good discard.

Sometimes the way to rectify the count is to duck in a suit where you have either one or two top winners. This play goes by the descriptive title of 'Submarine squeeze'.

```
              ♠ A Q 7 5
              ♡ K 6 4 2
              ◇ A J 4
              ♣ K 3

Contract: 6 NT
Lead:    ◇ 10

              ♠ K 6 2
              ♡ A Q 5 3
              ◇ K Q 8
              ♣ A 8 5
```

Obviously you have good chances in 6 NT – a 3–2 break in hearts or a 3–3 division of spades. But suppose the spades are 4–2 and the hearts 4–1: in that case your best chance will be to find the same opponent in charge of both suits. There might, theoretically, be a squeeze in clubs and one of the majors, but this is less likely and will be difficult to gauge during the play.

At the moment the timing is not right for a squeeze in the majors. Obviously you cannot duck a trick in spades or hearts, because in so doing you will destroy your menace card. The correct play, therefore, is to give up a club early on. This wins when the hand is of this type:

		♠ A Q 7 5		
		♡ K 6 4 2		
		◇ A J 4		
		♣ K 3		
♠ 10 4				♠ J 9 8 3
♡ 9				♡ J 10 8 7
◇ 10 9 7 6 2				◇ 5 3
♣ Q 10 7 4 2				♣ J 9 6
		♠ K 6 2		
		♡ A Q 5 3		
		◇ K Q 8		
		♣ A 8 5		

If you test the major suits in turn you will run into a blank wall. Instead, you must win the diamond lead and duck a club. After that, it is easy to squeeze East.

Another attractive way to restore the timing is to play loser on loser:

                    ♠ A Q 6
                    ♡ K 10 3
                    ◇ 7 6 4 2
                    ♣ K 6 3

♠ K J 9 5 2   ♠ 10 4
♡ 7 4 2   ♡ 8 5
◇ 9   ◇ A Q J 10 8 5
♣ Q J 7 2   ♣ 9 8 5

                    ♠ 8 7 3
                    ♡ A Q J 9 6
                    ◇ K 3
                    ♣ A 10 4

Southplays in Four Hearts after East has opened with a
pre-emptive Three Diamonds. West leads a diamond to the
Ace, ruffs the return and exits with a trump.

South can be fairly confident of the spade finesse, but he
is still a trick short. If he simply plays out winners he will be
left with a losing spade and a losing club. However, there is a
good chance that West will have exclusive control of both
black suits. At the moment the timing is wrong, but South
correct this with a neat play: after drawing trumps he leads a
third diamond from dummy and discards a spade from hand.
Say that East exits with a fourth diamond. South finesses
♠ Q, cashes the Ace and runs the trumps, arriving at this
position:

                    ♠ 6
                    ♡ —
                    ◇ —
                    ♣ K 6 3

♠ J   ♠ —
♡ —   ♡ —
◇ —   ◇ 10
♣ Q J 7   ♣ 9 8 5

                    ♠ —
                    ♡ Q
                    ◇ —
                    ♣ A 10 4

Now the last heart kills West.

Finally, it is often possible to force the opponents to improve your timing. This is a very common situation indeed in notrumps play:

<pre>
                        ♠ 10 6 4
                        ♡ A Q 5 2
                        ◇ K 9 4
                        ♣ K 8 2
    Contract: 3 NT
    Lead: ♠ 3

                        ♠ Q J 7
                        ♡ K 7 3
                        ◇ A 10 5 2
                        ♣ A 7 6
</pre>

West leads the 3 of spades against 3 NT and East contributes the 8. There are eight tricks on top. Perhaps the hearts will break 3–3, perhaps you can set up a ninth trick in diamonds. The obvious objection to giving up a diamond trick is that the opponents will then take four spade winners. Of course, the spades might be 4–3, but players do not normally lead fourth best from A K x x.

The only sensible play is to return a spade at once. If spades are 5–2, as is likely, you put West in a dilemma: if he cashes the spades he will give you perfect timing for a squeeze against East, and if he refrains from cashing all his winners you will probably be able to make the contract by giving up a diamond to East. You imagine the full hand to be something like this:

```
            ♠ 10 6 4
            ♡ A Q 5 2
            ◇ K 9 4
            ♣ K 8 2
♠ A K 9 3 2                    ♠ 8 5
♡ 10 4                         ♡ J 9 8 6
◇ 8 6 3                        ◇ Q J 7
♣ Q 10 5                       ♣ J 9 4 3
            ♠ Q J 7
            ♡ K 7 3
            ◇ A 10 5 2
            ♣ A 7 6
```

You win the first trick with ♠ Q and return a spade. West will know what you are trying to do and, as we shall see in Chapter 11, it might be good play on his part to refrain from cashing all his spades. However, this will not help on the present occasion, because you will be able to give up a diamond. If West does cash all his winners you discard a diamond and a club from dummy, a heart and a club from your own hand. East may let go three clubs, but then Ace and King of clubs will complete his discomfiture.

This type of squeeze is commonly known as a 'suicide squeeze' because the long suit played by one defender prepares the squeeze against his partner. 'Homicide squeeze' is a better description, because the player is squeezing his partner, not himself (though there are occasions when a defender should refrain from playing winners because this may lead to a squeeze against himself). Sometimes the eventual squeeze card is not one of declarer's winners but a loser which an opponent is forced to capture. This may happen without any special planning.

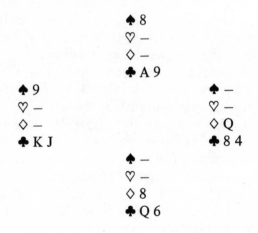

♠ 8 6 4 2
♡ 8 3
◊ J 6
♣ A 9 7 5 2

♠ A K J 9 5   ♠ 10 7
♡ 9 7   ♡ 10 6 5 2
◊ 10 5 2   ◊ Q 9 7 3
♣ K J 10   ♣ 8 4 3

♠ Q 3
♡ A K Q J 4
◊ A K 8 4
♠ Q 6

South played in Four Hearts after West had opened One Spade. West led ♠ K and followed with the Ace. On the third round East discarded a club and South ruffed. Declarer ruffed the third round of diamonds and drew trumps, arriving at this position:

♠ 8
♡ —
◊ —
♣ A 9

♠ 9   ♠ —
♡ —   ♡ —
◊ —   ◊ Q
♣ K J   ♣ 8 4

♠ —
♡ —
◊ 8
♣ Q 6

South led his losing diamond and West was the victim of a one-way squeeze, even though his partner won the trick.

6. Variations of the Simple Squeeze

In the last three chapters we have watched the declarer perform various manoeuvres to bring about one of the standard squeeze positions. In this chapter we study variations that will not reduce to the type of squeeze we have seen so far. These variations are not difficult and they occur quite often. In each case some expected component of the basic squeeze is missing but there is a compensating feature to restore the needs of the position.

Squeeze-without-the-count

As we have remarked more than once, the declarer will usually seek to reach a situation where he can win all the remaining tricks but one. However, this is not always possible and is by no means a necessary condition. Observe this simple four-card ending:

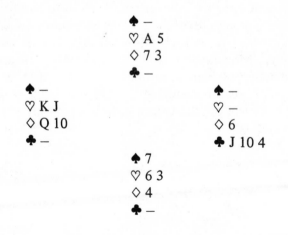

♠ —
♡ A 5
◇ 7 3
♣ —

♠ —
♡ K J
◇ Q 10
♣ —

♠ —
♡ —
◇ 6
♣ J 10 4

♠ 7
♡ 6 3
◇ 4
♣ —

South, playing either in notrumps or in spades, has only two winners and there are four cards left. However, it is quite simple to win an extra trick. On the 7 of spades West discards a diamond, North a heart, and then a diamond lead establishes a third winner.

Indeed, it is not uncommon for a defender to feel pressure early on and take several tricks later. We will see an example of that later in this chapter. For the moment we will concentrate on positions where just one trick is surrendered after the squeeze has begun. You may remember this deal from Chapter 2:

```
                              ♠ A 5
                              ♡ A K 6 2
                              ◇ Q 10 4 3
                              ♣ K 9 3
         Contract: 6 NT
         Lead:      ♠ K
                              ♠ J 8 4 3
                              ♡ Q 5
                              ◇ A K J 2
                              ♣ A Q J
```

You were advised to duck the opening lead to improve the timing. Then you played off the minor-suit winners, squeezing West, who began with ♠ K Q and four hearts. That is the best line of play, saving any guesses in the end-game, but suppose for a moment that you incautiously win the opening lead with dummy's Ace of spades. So long as you don't make the mistake of playing off the Queen of hearts early on, you can reach this ending:

                        ♠ 5
                        ♡ A K 6 2
                        ♢ 3
                        ♣ —

    ♠ Q 10
    ♡ J 9 7 4
    ♢ —   immaterial
    ♣ —

                        ♠ J 8 4
                        ♡ Q 5
                        ♢ J
                        ♣ —

When the last diamond is led West must throw a spade.
You give up a spade and make the rest of the tricks.

This was a second-best line of play, because West might
have kept different cards (such as ♠ Q 9 and ♡ J x x) and
forced you to take a view at the finish. Quite often, however,
it is not possible to rectify the count at an early stage. Here
South, playing in a pairs event, tried for a good score by
playing in 6 NT instead of the safer Six Diamonds:

                        ♠ K Q 7
                        ♡ 10 8 4
                        ♢ A 6 3
                        ♣ K J 9 2

    Contract: 6 NT
    Lead: ♡ K

                        ♠ A J 5 2
                        ♡ A
                        ♢ K 9 7 4 2
                        ♣ A Q 5

Prospects may not seem good when West leads the King of hearts, but the contract can be made if West holds ♡ K Q J and at least three diamonds. South must play spades first, because when the squeeze card (the fourth club) is led he must be in a position to exit with a heart, if necessary. He plays for this type of end position:

```
                        ♠ —
                        ♡ 10 8
                        ◇ A 6
                        ♣ J
      ♠ —
      ♡ Q J
      ◇ Q 10 3                      immaterial
      ♣ —
                        ♠ —
                        ♡ —
                        ◇ K 9 7 4 2
                        ♣ —
```

West is squeezed on the last club. Of course, declarer does not know at the beginning that West holds the diamond control, but he must make that assumption. Note that it was essential to retain top diamonds in both hands.

Any player might stumble on the ending shown above, but the next deal is a more searching test. Declarer will succeed only if he visualizes the ending and plays his cards in exactly the right order.

```
                        ♠ K 9 4
                        ♡ A 7 3
                        ◇ A Q J 6
                        ♣ 4 3 2
   Contract: 6 ♡
   Lead:      ♠ Q
                        ♠ A 5 3
                        ♡ K Q J 10 4
                        ◇ K 7 2
                        ♣ K 8
```

62

West, who has opened One Spade, leads the Queen of spades against your contract of Six Hearts. West is marked with the Ace of clubs, so at first sight you seem doomed to lose either a spade and a club or two clubs. However, that is not so: if West has control of both black suits you can torment him. But do you see the right sequence of play?

You expect the end position to be:

```
                    ♠ K 9
                    ♡ —
                    ◊ —
                    ♣ 4 3
    ♠ J 10
    ♡ —                             immaterial
    ◊ —
    ♣ A Q
                    ♠ 5
                    ♡ 10
                    ◊ —
                    ♣ K 8
```

On the lead of the 10 of hearts West must bare the Ace of clubs. You discard a spade from dummy and exit with a low club, establishing a trick for the King of clubs.

The squeeze is one-way and the squeeze card must come from South. This brings us to the heart of the matter: you must play off diamonds before hearts, and to retain an entry to hand you must keep a third heart in dummy, despite the possibility of a ruff. The full hand is:

```
                    ♠ K 9 4
                    ♡ A 7 3
                    ♢ A Q J 6
                    ♣ 4 3 2
      ♠ Q J 10 7 6 2              ♠ 8
      ♡ 9 5                       ♡ 8 6 2
      ♢ 8                         ♢ 10 9 5 4 3
      ♣ A Q J 6                   ♣ 10 9 7 5
                    ♠ A 5 3
                    ♡ K Q J 10 4
                    ♢ K 7 2
                    ♣ K 8
```

The sequence of play in Six Hearts is: win with ♠ K A, draw two trumps with King and Ace, play four diamonds, throwing a spade, return to hand with the third trump and play off the remaining hearts. As we remarked earlier, you will not make this type of contract unless you know what you are trying to do!

Criss-cross squeeze

A squeeze-without-the-count occurs when it is not practicable to rectify the timing; a criss-cross squeeze when there is no controlling card in the hand of the two-card menace. Instead of holding, for example, Q x opposite A x, a typical divided menace, you have a blocked position, Q x opposite a singleton Ace. To make anything of this, you need the same sort of combination in two suits, as in this ending:

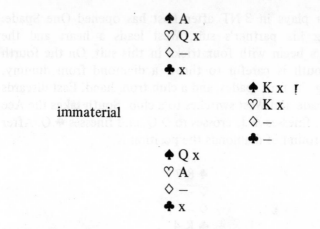

immaterial

When the winning club is played, East has no good discard. This is an automatic squeeze, so it doesn't matter whether the top club is in the North or South hand. Criss-cross squeezes are not particularly common and are often vulnerable to an assault on entry cards, but they need to be understood because they may come to the declarer's aid when he has awkward combinations such as J x x opposite A K alone, or Q x x opposite A J alone. On this deal the declarer's spade combination is the sign that a criss-cross may be needed:

```
                    ♠ 8 7 4 2
                    ♡ 9 5 3
                    ◇ Q 6 2
                    ♣ A K 4
    ♠ 5                         ♠ K 10 9 6 3
    ♡ Q J 10 7                  ♡ A K 2
    ◇ 9 7 5 4 3                 ◇ J 8
    ♣ 8 6 2                     ♣ Q 10 5
                    ♠ A Q J
                    ♡ 8 6 4
                    ◇ A K 10
                    ♣ J 9 7 3
```

South plays in 3 NT after East has opened One Spade. Spurning his partner's suit, West leads a heart and the defenders begin with four tricks in this suit. On the fourth heart South is careful to throw a diamond from dummy, retaining the four spades, and a club from hand. East discards a low spade and West switches to a club. South takes the Ace of clubs, finesses ♠ J, crosses to ◊ Q, and finesses ♠ Q. After another round of diamonds the position is:

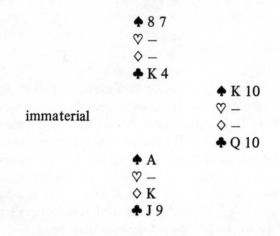

```
              ♠ 8 7
              ♡ —
              ◊ —
              ♣ K 4
                              ♠ K 10
                              ♡ —
  immaterial                  ◊ —
                              ♣ Q 10
              ♠ A
              ♡ —
              ◊ K
              ♣ J 9
```

On the King of diamonds a club is thrown from dummy and East is caught in a criss-cross. South cannot go wrong in the end-game because he has a sure count of the spade suit.

On this deal the declarer has a choice between a criss-cross and the play for a 3–3 break in clubs:

```
              ♠ A Q 3
              ♡ 9 8 4
              ◊ A 10 5
              ♣ 8 7 4 2
Contract: 3 NT
Lead:     ♠ 6
              ♠ 10 7 5 2
              ♡ J 10 7 2
              ◊ K 8
              ♣ A K Q
```

South plays in 3 NT and West leads the 6 of spades. Declarer plays low from dummy and East wins with the Jack. He returns a low heart; the Jack loses to the Queen and West returns a heart to his partner's King. It is good play now to drop the 7 or 10, encouraging East to cash the Ace. East does so, and West discards a diamond. East exits with a club. After a spade finesse and another top club, to which all follow, the position is:

♠ A
♡ —
◇ A 10 5
♣ 8 7

♠ 10 7
♡ 10
◇ K 8
♣ Q

South needs the rest of the tricks. He cashes the 10 of hearts; West parts with another diamond and dummy discards ◇ 5.

At this point an inexpert declarer would cash the Queen of clubs, playing for a 3–3 break. A better player would reflect on these lines:

'No doubt West has K x of spades left. If anyone has four clubs it is likely to be West, because with 4-2-5-2 distribution he would probably have led a diamond. There is no need to test the clubs at once. I can play off the top diamonds to get a better count of the West hand'.

If West (who has thrown two diamonds, remember) follows to the Ace and King it may be presumed that he began with 4-2-4-3 distribution. But if West instead was 4-2-3-4 he will be forced to unguard one of the black suits on the second round of diamonds. This was the full hand:

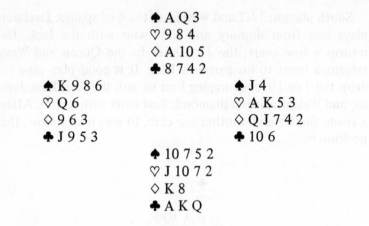

East's heart switch at trick two was reasonable play, but the contract could have been defeated if he had returned a spade. When West came in with the Queen of hearts he would play a third round of spades, destroying a necessary entry for the criss-cross.

Trump squeeze

We look next at the trump (or ruffing) squeeze, because this is a first cousin of the criss-cross. A trump performs the function of one of the top controls necessary in a criss-cross squeeze.

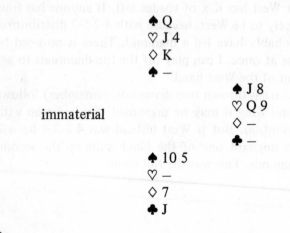

At notrumps South would not be able to develop an extra trick, but clubs are trumps and he leads a diamond to the King. Now East must unguard one of the majors and South has the necessary entries to take advantage. Whereas in a criss-cross the declarer always has a single control in each hand, here he has a trump in his own hand instead.

Two entries are always needed in the hand opposite the trumps. In the example above the second entry is in a third suit, diamonds; it may alternatively be in a suit that the declarer is seeking to establish.

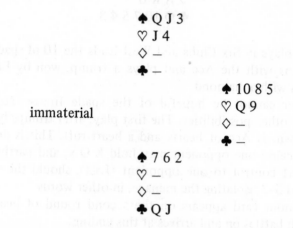

Again clubs are trumps and now the penultimate trump applies the pressure. North throws a spade and East is squeezed.

A trump squeeze is always automatic but is played more often against the right-hand opponent, because when the left-hand opponent holds the critical cards a simple squeeze will usually be playable. The indications, therefore, are: menace cards in two suits held by the right-hand opponent, no possibility of a straightforward squeeze, at least two quick entries to the dummy after trumps have been drawn.

```
        ♠ K J 5
        ♡ A J 7 3
        ◇ Q 5 2
        ♣ K J 9
♠ 10 9              ♠ Q 8 7 6 4
♡ K 9 2             ♡ Q 10 8 5 4
◇ 10 8 7 4 3        ◇ J 9
♣ 8 6 2            ♣ A
        ♠ A 3 2
        ♡ 6
        ◇ A K 6
        ♣ Q 10 7 5 4 3
```

South plays in Six Clubs and West leads the 10 of spades. South wins with the Ace and plays a trump, won by East, who exits with a diamond.

Declarer cannot be hopeful of the spade finesse, so he looks for other possibilities. The first play, after trumps have been drawn, is Ace of hearts and a heart ruff. This is done partly because one opponent may hold K Q x, and partly to limit heart control to one opponent (East), should the suit be divided 5–3; isolating the menace, in other words.

No honour card appears on the second round of hearts, but South battles on and arrives at this ending:

```
        ♠ K J
        ♡ J 7
        ◇ Q
        ♣ —
♠ 9                 ♠ Q 8
♡ K                 ♡ Q 10 8
◇ 10 8 7            ◇ —
♣ —                ♣ —
        ♠ 3 2
        ♡ —
        ◇ 6
        ♣ 10 7
```

On the 10 of clubs a spade is thrown from dummy and East can afford a heart. Then a diamond to the Queen slays East.

The trump squeeze is perhaps more difficult to foresee on this type of hand, where the extra trick is developed after a ruffing finesse in dummy's long suit:

```
                    ♠ 8 6 3
                    ♡ A Q 10 5 2
                    ◇ 8 4
                    ♣ A 5 2
  ♠ A K 10 7 2                    ♠ J 9 5
  ♡ 8 6 3                         ♡ K 9 7 4
  ◇ 10 7 2                        ◇ J 5
  ♣ J 10                          ♣ Q 9 6 3
                    ♠ Q 4
                    ♡ J
                    ◇ A K Q 9 6 3
                    ♣ K 8 7 4
```

South plays in Five Diamonds and West begins with two top spades. When he sees that there is no possibility of a third trick in spades, West switches to the Jack of clubs. (This is good play, because otherwise declarer would be able to establish one extra heart by a ruffing finesse and then negotiate a straightforward squeeze against East in the minor suits.)

After West has turned up with ♠ A K South is disposed to place East with the King of hearts. A ruffing finesse will establish one extra trick, but where will the other come from?

At any rate, South must win the club in hand with the King and draw trumps. On the third trump East completes a peter in clubs, and on the fourth trump he parts with the Jack of spades. The position is now:

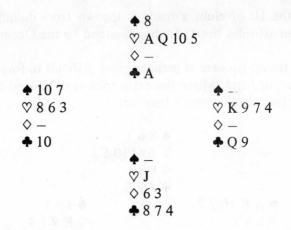

                              ♠ 8
                              ♥ A Q 10 5
                              ◇ —
                              ♣ A
        ♠ 10 7   ♠ —
        ♥ 8 6 3   ♥ K 9 7 4
        ◇ —   ◇ —
        ♣ 10   ♣ Q 9
                              ♠ —
                              ♥ J
                              ◇ 6 3
                              ♣ 8 7 4

On the next diamond a spade is thrown from dummy and East is under the hammer. If he lets go a heart, then declarer can establish two extra winners in this suit.

Another, quite simple type of ruffing squeeze occurs when a defender who has length in two side suits is forced to unguard one of them when discarding on trump leads.

                              ♠ A 9 8 2
                              ♥ 5 3
                              ◇ 8 6 4 3
                              ♣ 9 7 2
        ♠ 10 7 4   ♠ Q J 6 3
        ♥ Q 10 6   ♥ J 9 4 2
        ◇ J 10 5   ◇ 9
        ♣ Q J 10 4   ♣ A K 6 5
                              ♠ K 5
                              ♥ A K 8 7
                              ◇ A K Q 7 2
                              ♣ 8 3

Playing in Five Diamonds, South ruffs the third round of clubs and cashes ◇ A K, East discarding his fourth club. Rather than try to ruff two hearts in dummy, South should realize that East is quite possibly 4-4-1-4 and will be inconvenienced by a third round of trumps. South will be able to ruff out a winner in whichever suit East unguards.

There is also the 'See-saw' or 'Overtaking' squeeze, where the declarer, with two trumps in each hand, overtakes or not according to the discard of the next player. We give an example of this in Chapter 10.

Squeeze and throw-in

The writers of textbooks tend to treat squeezes and throw-ins as separate creatures, but there is undoubtedly a squeeze element in the preparation for the majority of throw-in plays. Consider this familiar type of deal:

```
                 ♠ 10 4
                 ♡ Q 6 5
                 ◇ K J 9 6 2
                 ♣ J 7 4
♠ A Q 9 7 6 3                    ♠ J 5
♡ K 10 4                         ♡ J 9 3 2
◇ 10 3                           ◇ 8 5 4
♣ 9 2                            ♣ K Q 8 3
                 ♠ K 8 2
                 ♡ A 8 7
                 ◇ A Q 7
                 ♣ A 10 6 5
```

South plays in 3 NT and West leads a low spade, which is covered by the Jack and King. After four rounds of diamonds the position will be something like this:

```
                    ♠ 10
                    ♡ Q 6 5
                    ◇ 9
                    ♣ J 7 4
   ♠ A Q 9 6 3                      ♠ 5
   ♡ K 10                           ♡ J 9 3 2
   ◇ —                              ◇ —
   ♣ 9                              ♣ K Q 3
                    ♠ 8 2
                    ♡ A 8 7
                    ◇ —
                    ♣ A 10
```

On the last diamond South discards a spade and West is under pressure. If he lets go a spade, South can play Ace and another heart, so he may decide to throw a club; then the Ace of clubs forces him to throw a spade and leaves him open to a throw-in. It is true that if West discards in a fluent and deceptive way he may escape this fate, but many contracts are made by this kind of play.

It is easier for the declarer to judge the lie of the cards on this next hand because if his original assumptions are correct he needs to determine the division of only one suit:

```
                    ♠ A Q 5
                    ♡ J 7
                    ◇ 8 6 4 3
                    ♣ A Q 6 3

Contract: 6 ♠
Lead:     ♡ K
                    ♠ K J 10 8 3
                    ♡ A 5
                    ◇ A Q
                    ♣ K J 7 2
```

74

South plays in Six Spades after West has made a vulnerable overcall of Two Hearts. Declarer must assume that the diamond finesse is wrong and after the lead of ♡ K there are two possible lines of play. A partial elimination might succeed: win with ♡ A, draw two trumps only, cash two clubs and exit in hearts. If West has no more clubs or spades he will be 'on play'.

However, a combination of squeeze and throw-in is more promising. Declarer plays off all the black cards, reducing to ♡ 5 and ◇ A Q. So long as he has been able to read the heart distribution he will know whether West has kept ♡ Q and ◇ K x or has trickily come down to ♡ Q x and ◇ K alone. Generally speaking, the player to watch is East. Most defenders, with the best of intentions, will attempt to give their partners the count; for example, by playing high–low with an even number. So as declarer you must be careful to note the heart pips played by East.

Show-up squeeze

Finally, there is a type of squeeze where the defender is not forced to discard a winner but is forced to expose a significant card in his partner's hand. This is known variously as a discovery, information, or show-up squeeze.

South dealer
East–West vulnerable

	♠ A Q 9 5	
	♡ J 9 4	
	◇ 9 5 3 2	
	♣ K 6	
♠ 10 8 7 4 3 2		♠ K
♡ 6		♡ A 8 5
◇ J 10 8 7		◇ A K Q
♣ Q 2		♣ J 8 7 5 4 3
	♠ J 6	
	♡ K Q 10 7 3 2	
	◇ 6 4	
	♣ A 10 9	

South	West	North	East
1♡	No	1♠	No
2♡	No	4♡	No
No	No		

West leads ◇ J and the defence begins with three rounds of this suit. South ruffs and leads a low heart to the Jack. When East holds off, South takes his club ruff and leads another trump. East wins and exits with a club, which South ruffs.

Most declarers would draw the last heart and announce the spade finesse, but this would be an error. South should continue trumps, arriving at this position:

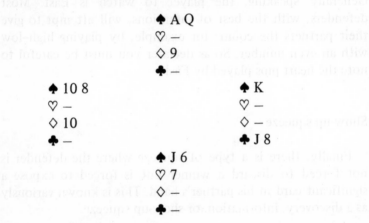

On the last heart West discards a spade, North a diamond, and East a club. When West follows to the spade on the next trick South knows the finesse cannot succeed, because West's remaining card is undoubtedly the 10 of diamonds. So South goes up with the Ace of spades and drops the singleton King, to the annoyance of the opposition.

7. Squeezing Both Opponents

A boxer takes on one adversary at a time. A follower of kung-fu is more ambitious: he expects his hero to tackle all opponents in a single bout. And you can do this at the bridge table if you understand the operation of a double squeeze. The basic requirements are similar to those for a simple squeeze, but like the kung-fu fighter you will need to keep an eye on both opponents. The squeeze can operate – and very often does – in a three-card ending:

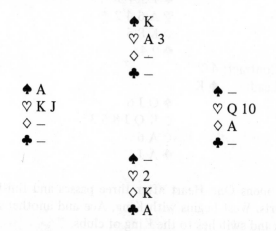

♠ K
♡ A 3
◇ –
♣ –

♠ A
♡ K J
◇ –
♣ –

♠ –
♡ Q 10
◇ A
♣ –

♠ –
♡ 2
◇ K
♣ A

When South plays off the Ace of clubs each defender is squeezed in turn. West, playing in front of dummy, must keep his winning spade, so he discards a heart. Dummy's King of spades, having done a valuable turn of duty, is permitted to retire. Now East, in sole control of both red suits, cannot withstand the pressure.

Let us examine the components of this position:

1   Declarer has a threat in each of three suits and a squeeze card in the fourth.
2   Each defender controls one of the single menaces, and both menaces are well placed for the declarer. That is to say, in the example above, the spade King is 'over' West and the diamond King is 'over' East.
3   The two-card menace, with which we are very familiar, is controlled by both opponents. The suit in which the two-card menace is held is called the 'pivot suit'.

It is not at all difficult to foresee the chance for a double squeeze. You look for two well-placed menace cards and for a third suit that both opponents are likely to control.

$$\spadesuit\ 7\ 5\ 4\ 3$$
$$\heartsuit\ A\ 6\ 4\ 2$$
$$\diamondsuit\ K\ 8\ 5$$
$$\clubsuit\ 9\ 4$$

Contract: 4 $\heartsuit$
Lead: $\spadesuit$ K

$$\spadesuit\ Q\ J\ 6$$
$$\heartsuit\ K\ Q\ J\ 8\ 5\ 3$$
$$\diamondsuit\ A\ 6$$
$$\clubsuit\ A\ J$$

South opens One Heart after three passes and finishes in Four Hearts. West begins with King, Ace and another spade. East ruffs and switches to the King of clubs.

You can almost put down your cards. You know that dummy's last spade is a menace against West, and unless East is playing a funny sort of game your Jack of clubs will be a menace against his Queen. So, how will they both guard diamonds? You play for this ending:

78

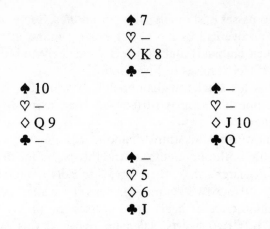

```
            ♠ 7
            ♡ —
            ◇ K 8
            ♣ —
♠ 10                      ♠ —
♡ —                       ♡ —
◇ Q 9                     ◇ J 10
♣ —                       ♣ Q
            ♠ —
            ♡ 5
            ◇ 6
            ♣ J
```

Note that it is not even necessary to keep a close count of the diamonds. When the last heart is led West must keep the 10 of spades, so you part with dummy's 7 and need only to observe whether East discards a diamond or the Queen of clubs.

In this next deal we meet our old friend, 'isolating the menace':

```
                    ♠ A 7 4 3
                    ♡ 10 7 5 2
                    ◇ 9 8 5
                    ♣ K J
♠ J 10 8 2                          ♠ Q 9 5
♡ K J 9 6 3                         ♡ Q 8 4
◇ 2                                 ◇ A Q J 10 7 3
♣ 10 6 2                            ♣ 5
                    ♠ K 6
                    ♡ A
                    ◇ K 6 4
                    ♣ A Q 9 8 7 4 3
```

After two passes East opens Three Diamonds. Some players would risk an overcall of 3 NT, but this is somewhat unsafe with a broken club suit and South is more likely to bid Four Clubs, which North raises to Five Clubs.

West leads his singleton diamond. East wins and returns the Queen. South's King is ruffed and West exits with the Jack of spades.

South knows that his third diamond is a menace against East. Probably both opponents control the spades and hearts – at present. Declarer's task, therefore, is to isolate the menace in hearts by ruffing two rounds. He wins the spade lead with the King, cashes Ace of hearts, and crosses to dummy twice in clubs to ruff two hearts. Then he arrives at this ending:

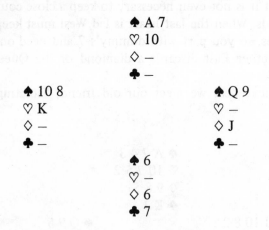

The last club squeezes both opponents.

This would have been a still more interesting hand to play if North's clubs had been K 10 instead of K J. Despite the risk of looking foolish, it would be good play to finesse the 10 of clubs on the first round, to obtain the necessary entries for two heart ruffs.

80

When both one-card menaces are in the same hand

When the menaces are not ideally placed, some form of compensation will be needed. In this section we look at situations where both one-card menaces are in the same hand. The minimum compass is four cards and these must be compensation in the form of extra control in the pivot suit:

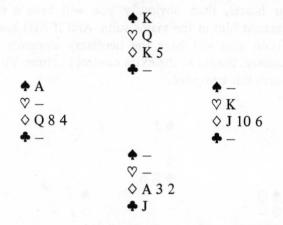

Here the two one-card menaces, the King of spades and the Queen of hearts, are both in the North hand. Nevertheless, the squeeze works because of the double-entry menace in diamonds. The term 'double-entry menace' means that there is a control in each hand. On the Jack of clubs West throws a diamond, North a spade, and East is squeezed.

See how quickly you can find the answer to this deal:

```
              ♠ A J 6
              ♡ A Q 7 5 2
              ◇ K 8
              ♣ K 6 5

Contract: 7 NT
Lead:     ♠ K

              ♠ 4
              ♡ K 8 6
              ◇ A Q J 10 3 2
              ♣ A 4 2
```

Playing for a top score in a pairs, you finish in 7 NT rather than Seven Diamonds, a safer contract because you would be able to ruff the fourth round of hearts if necessary.

Against 7 NT West leads the King of spades. Now, assuming West has the Queen of spades, the contract is a certainty. Do you see why?

Early on you play Ace and King of hearts. If West began with four hearts, then obviously you will have a simple squeeze against him in the major suits. And if East has four hearts? Then you will have the necessary elements for a double squeeze, thanks to the extra control in clubs. You will steer towards this end-game:

```
                    ♠ J
                    ♡ 7
                    ◇ —
                    ♣ K 6
  ♠ Q                               ♠ —
  ♡ —                               ♡ J
  ◇ —                               ◇ —
  ♣ J 9 7                           ♣ Q 10 8
                    ♠ —
                    ♡ —
                    ◇ 3
                    ♣ A 4 2
```

The last diamond squeezes both opponents in turn.

Alternatively, the two one-card menaces may be in the same hand as the squeeze card. This is possible when there is an extension to the two-card menace, as in this ending:

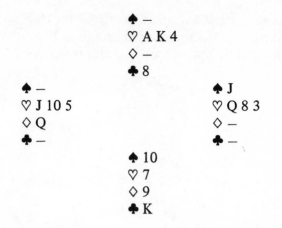

Dummy's hearts in this example are known as a 'recessed menace'. The two controls, opposite the singleton, allow room for two one-card menaces to lurk in the South hand. When the King of clubs is led, each defender must set up a winner for south or abandon the hearts.

A recessed menace is always a pleasing sight for the declarer, because his chance of finding one opponent in charge of two suits is greatly increased. This is a common type of hand:

♠ K 10 6
♡ A K Q 2
◇ A 8 3
♣ 8 7 5

Contract: 6 ♠
Lead: ♣ 4

♠ A Q J 8 5 3
♡ 7 4
◇ Q 6
♣ A J 3

West leads the 4 of clubs against Six Spades and East plays the King. South could take this trick and play for a throw-in against an opponent holding Queen of clubs and King of diamonds, but there is a stronger line. Duck the club, win the likely club return, cash the Ace of diamonds (a *Vienna Coup*), then run the spades. You will arrive at this position:

♠ —
♡ A K Q 2
◇ —
♣ 8

♠ J
♡ 7 4
◇ Q
♣ J

You succeed now so long as the opponent who has the long hearts has *either* King of diamonds *or* Queen of clubs. This is not strictly a double squeeze, it is true, because only one opponent can hold the hearts, but both opponents are involved and the example shows the value of a recessed menace.

In many cases a recessed menace (similarly, a double menace) is open to attack by the defender. On this next deal the defenders have little choice because they are obliged to lead a trump:

```
                    ♠ A Q 7 3
                    ♡ 9 7 4
                    ◇ K Q 8 4
                    ♣ 6 5
♠ K J 8 4                           ♠ 10 9 5 2
♡ A Q 3                             ♡ 6
◇ J 10                              ◇ A 9 6 5
♣ Q 10 7 3                          ♣ 9 8 4 2
                    ♠ 6
                    ♡ K J 10 8 5 2
                    ◇ 7 3 2
                    ♣ A K J
```

South plays in Four Hearts after West has opened with a weak notrump. West leads the Jack of diamonds and the Queen is played from dummy. East might consider holding off, but this wouldn't help on the present occasion because South could obtain an early discard by finessing in spades; he would then ruff a club and give up two trump tricks.

So let us say that East wins the first diamond. A spade return now would damage the entries, but East is obliged to lead a trump to prevent a club ruff. Following this line of defence, West plays a second and third round of trumps.

At this point South expects the spade finesse to win, but not the club finesse, especially when East discards low clubs. South must lay down the Queen of diamonds, establishing the 7 as a menace against East, and play off all the trumps to produce this ending:

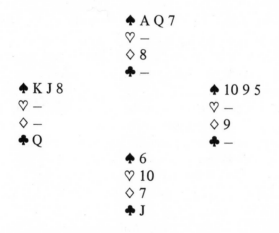

The two one-card menaces (you cannot count the 8 of diamonds) are in the same hand, but the squeeze works because of the recessed menace in spades.

Non-simultaneous double squeeze

In all the examples we have looked at so far the squeeze has operated on a single trick. Sometimes the opponents are squeezed on different tricks. Here South is playing in notrumps:

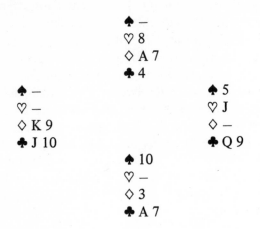

```
              ♠ —
              ♡ 8
              ◊ A 7
              ♣ 4
  ♠ —                    ♠ 5
  ♡ —                    ♡ J
  ◊ K 9                  ◊ —
  ♣ J 10                 ♣ Q 9
              ♠ 10
              ♡ —
              ◊ 3
              ♣ A 7
```

South leads the 10 of spades. Because of the diamond threat West must let go a club. Dummy discards the 7 of diamonds, which has done its work. East is not squeezed on this trick – indeed, he follows suit; but a diamond to the Ace now defeats him.

This non-simultaneous squeeze occurs when the double menace is in the same hand as the squeeze card. To compensate, there must be a second two-card menace. Those conditions exist here:

```
              ♠ K Q 6 3
              ♡ 7 4 2
              ◊ Q 9 5
              ♣ J 6 3
  ♠ J 9 5 4              ♠ 10 7 2
  ♡ J 8 6                ♡ Q 10 5 3
  ◊ 8 7 6                ◊ A J 10 2
  ♣ 9 5 2                ♣ 8 4
              ♠ A 8
              ♡ A K 9
              ◊ K 4 3
              ♣ A K Q 10 7
```

86

South is in 6 NT and West leads the 8 of diamonds. It is good play to go up with the Queen, forcing East to part with the Ace and so rectifying the count. East will probably return the Jack of diamonds to South's King.

South is confident that dummy's 9 of diamonds is a menace against East and he must assume that West holds the spades. There is a double menace in hearts, and as the entry to the hand opposite the squeeze card, ♣ 7, is in the same suit as one of the single menaces, the squeeze will be non-simultaneous (or successive, if you want a simple description). This is the position after four rounds of clubs:

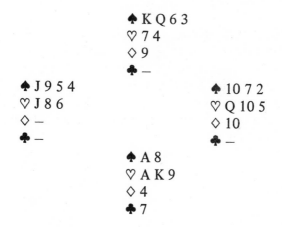

```
              ♠ K Q 6 3
              ♡ 7 4
              ♢ 9
              ♣ —
♠ J 9 5 4                    ♠ 10 7 2
♡ J 8 6                      ♡ Q 10 5
♢ —                          ♢ 10
♣ —                          ♣ —
              ♠ A 8
              ♡ A K 9
              ♢ 4
              ♣ 7
```

West feels the pressure on the next club: he must let go a heart. East, not troubled at the moment, discards a spade, but then three rounds of spades are more than he can bear.

These non-simultaneous squeezes often occur at the table because the declarer has followed a particular sequence of play.

```
            ♠ K 6 4
            ♡ 7 5 2
            ♢ A K 6
            ♣ K J 6 3
♠ Q 7 3                      ♠ J 9 5 2
♡ K J 9 6 4                  ♡ A 8
♢ 8                          ♢ Q 10 5 3 2
♣ Q 9 8 2                    ♣ 10 7
            ♠ A 10 8
            ♡ Q 10 3
            ♢ J 9 7 4
            ♣ A 5 4
```

North, playing a strong notrump, opens One Club and
South responds 2 NT. Quite rightly taking a gloomy view of
his unproductive assortment, North passes.

West leads a heart and the defenders take their tricks in
this suit. (West may hesitate to cash the fifth heart because of
the danger of a squeeze, but in this case declarer will establish
a trick in diamonds.)

The last round of hearts forces South to part with a
diamond. The players will probably keep these cards:

```
            ♠ K 6
            ♡ —
            ♢ A K
            ♣ K J 6 3
♠ Q 7 3                      ♠ J 9 5
♡ —                          ♡ —
♢ 8                          ♢ Q 10 5
♣ Q 9 8 2                    ♣ 10 7
            ♠ A 10 8
            ♡ —
            ♢ J 9 7
            ♣ A 5
```

West exits with a diamond to the Ace and declarer cashes the King. This wrings a spade from West. After the Ace of clubs and a finesse of the Jack, the King of clubs squeezes East.

It may be observed that on this occasion the squeeze card, the King of diamonds, is not in the same hand as the double menace (♠ A 10 8). The explanation for this is that the declarer has played his cards in a particular order. It suited him to test the diamonds early. He might, instead, have won with ♢ A, played a club to the Ace, finessed the Jack, and cashed the two black Kings. Then the King of diamonds would have been the squeeze card in a classical three-card ending.

It is worth noting, as a fact of life, that a double menace and a two-card menace opposite a hand containing a squeeze card and a well-placed single menace will always supply the ingredients for a squeeze. You may test that proposition by relating it to the following deal:

```
                    ♠ A 10 5
                    ♡ J 8 7 4
                    ♢ A K 3
                    ♣ 7 4 2
    ♠ J 9 7 4 3                     ♠ Q 8 2
    ♡ 6 2                           ♡ A
    ♢ 10 8 7 4                      ♢ Q J 9 5
    ♣ 6 5                           ♣ K J 10 8 3
                    ♠ K 6
                    ♡ K Q 10 9 5 3
                    ♢ 6 2
                    ♣ A Q 9
```

South plays in Six Hearts after East has opened One Club. West leads the 6 of clubs and South wins the first trick with the Queen. When he comes in with ♡ A East's best return, as the cards lie, is a spade, but that is difficult to judge and he will probably try another club. South may play off one of the diamond honours but must not touch the spades. After one diamond and four rounds of trumps he arrives at this position:

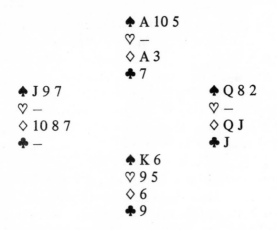

♠ A 10 5
♡ —
♢ A 3
♣ 7

♠ J 9 7
♡ —
♢ 10 8 7
♣ —

♠ Q 8 2
♡ —
♢ Q J
♣ J

♠ K 6
♡ 9 5
♢ 6
♣ 9

Both opponents control both the two-card menaces, but the squeeze cannot be defended. On the 9 of hearts West can spare a diamond and dummy a club. What can East throw? If a diamond, South can cross to ♢ A, return to ♠ K, and lead the last trump. East's best discard on ♡ 9 is a spade. Now declarer must take Ace and King of spades before leading the 5 of hearts in a typical double squeeze position.

Concluding this subject, you will often hear players claim to have executed a 'triple squeeze'. If you adopt the terminology we have used, the phrase 'triple squeeze' has no meaning.

8. Two Tricks from a Squeeze

Let us, for a moment, review progress. We have examined so far:

The SIMPLE Squeeze, where there are two menace cards lying against a single opponent; and

The DOUBLE squeeze, where there are two single menaces, one against each opponent, and a pivot suit which both control.

Each of these types, even in the more complicated variations, gains only one trick. The third type, the subject of this chapter, is:

The PROGRESSIVE squeeze, where there are menaces against one opponent in each of three suits and TWO TRICKS are gained.

How can this be? It is like the style of warfare in which conquered territory is used as the base for a further attack. Having squeezed an opponent out of a winner, you cash your own newly established trick and squeeze him again.

To achieve this happy result, you need either a specially favourable arrangement of menaces or a slightly less favourable arrangement backed by an 'extended menace'. An extended menace occurs when an opponent cannot unguard a suit without surrendering at least two tricks. For example, a defender who holds K x over dummy's A Q J is liable to give away two tricks if he bares the King.

We will look first at endings where there is no extended menace. To win two tricks from a squeeze now, you need:

A two-card menace in each hand;
A one-card menace on the right side of, i.e. over, the victim.

The minimum compass for this squeeze is five cards:

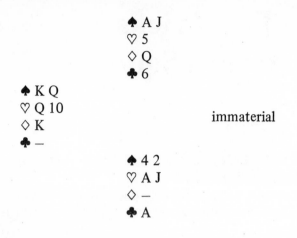

♠ A J
♡ 5
◇ Q
♣ 6

♠ K Q
♡ Q 10   immaterial
◇ K
♣ —

♠ 4 2
♡ A J
◇ —
♣ A

You see here that you have the requirements mentioned above: two-card menaces in the major suits and a favourably positioned one-card menace, the Queen of diamonds; and, of course, a squeeze card in clubs. West must give up a trick when ♣ A is led, and a second squeeze follows.

Note that this squeeze will not work if declarer weakens his assets by playing off a control in a two-card menace before the squeeze card. For example, suppose he plays off ♡ A before the Ace of clubs: then West will defeat the progressive squeeze by discarding a spade on ♣ A, giving up one trick but not two. Discarding against a threatened squeeze of this kind is a separate problem, which we discuss in Chapter 11.

The squeeze shown above is one way. It would not operate if you transferred the West cards to East, because East would throw a heart now, again giving declarer just one extra trick.

To achieve a progressive squeeze against the opponent on your right you will need the one-card menace to be in your own hand, sitting over the victim:

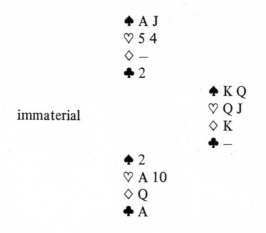

♠ A J
♡ 5 4
◇ –
♣ 2

immaterial

♠ K Q
♡ Q J
◇ K
♣ –

♠ 2
♡ A 10
◇ Q
♣ A

The progressive squeeze in this diagram would not work against West.

To repeat a warning given in the first chapter, do not imagine that it is a waste of time to study these situations from a theoretical angle. If you don't begin that way, you will never know what you are doing or what to look for, what assumptions you need to make, or in what order to play the cards. No doubt, however, you are ready now to look at a full deal:

♠ 10 4 2
♡ A Q 7 3
◇ K 8 3
♣ Q 6 4

♠ K Q J 8
♡ J 10 8 2
◇ Q J 6
♣ 9 7

♠ 7 6 5
♡ 9 4
◇ 9 7 4 2
♣ 10 5 3 2

♠ A 9 3
♡ K 6 5
◇ A 10 5
♣ A K J 8

South is in 6 NT and West leads the King of spades. South can see ten tricks on top and a 3–3 break in hearts would provide an eleventh. In any case he will duck the first trick to rectify the count and make the subsequent play easier. West continues with the Queen of spades. South wins and plays off three rounds of clubs, discarding a diamond from dummy. The position is now:

<pre>
                    ♠ 10
                    ♡ A Q 7 3
                    ◇ K 8 3
                    ♣ —
    ♠ J
    ♡ J 10 8 2
    ◇ Q J 6   immaterial
    ♣ —
                    ♠ 9
                    ♡ K 6 5
                    ◇ A 10 5
                    ♣ J
</pre>

The last club destroys West. He must give up a trick now and another trick when the winner is cashed in whatever suit he unguards.

Note that the squeeze would not work in the same way if South were to play off three rounds of hearts. The ending would be:

<pre>
                    ♠ 10
                    ♡ 7
                    ◇ K 8 3
                    ♣ —
    ♠ J
    ♡ J
    ◇ Q J 6   immaterial
    ♣ —
                    ♠ 9
                    ♡ —
                    ◇ A 10 5
                    ♣ J
</pre>

South still has three menaces against West, but he has squandered one of his two-card menaces. Even so, West must be careful to make the right discard on the Jack of clubs: he must throw a diamond to escape a second squeeze.

The progressive squeeze on this deal would work equally well if the East and West hands were exchanged. This is because South's 9 of spades would be a one-card menace against East; but if South's spades were A 5 3 instead of A 9 x, there would not be the necessary conditions for a progressive squeeze against the right-hand opponent.

See how theoretical knowledge will guide you to the best line of play with these cards:

♠ Q 4
♡ A Q 6
◇ A K 10 4
♣ K Q 5 3

Contract: 7 NT
Lead:　　♡ 10

♠ A K 7 3
♡ K J 8
◇ 7 6 5 2
♣ A 4

At rubber bridge South opened One Spade and North forced with Three Clubs. When South rebid 3 NT North launched the 'old Black'. Having discovered that his side held all the Aces and Kings, he saw no bar to a final contract of 7 NT.

West led the 10 of hearts and South could count no more than eleven tricks on top. Consider carefully: what must he hope to find? How should he begin? Try to answer before looking at the full deal:

```
                    ♠ Q 4
                    ♡ A Q 6
                    ◇ A K 10 4
                    ♣ K Q 5 3
♠ 10 6 5                          ♠ J 9 8 2
♡ 10 9 7 5 3                      ♡ 4 2
◇ Q 8                            ◇ J 9 3
♣ 10 9 6                         ♣ J 8 7 2
                    ♠ A K 7 3
                    ♡ K J 8
                    ◇ 7 6 5 2
                    ♣ A 4
```

It seemed to the declarer that the only hope lay in finding a lucky division in diamonds. He won the first trick with the King of hearts and finessed ◇ 10 – to the great relief of one of the present authors, who held the East cards and was wondering desperately what he would discard if South began with three rounds of hearts.

South should have summed the position in this way: 'I have eleven tricks on top. There is a chance of a progressive squeeze if either defender is 4-2-3-4 and so must guard menaces in three suits. I can finesse the 10 of diamonds later. First, I'll try the effect of three rounds of hearts.'

East's best chance, as it happens, is to throw a club on the third heart. If East can do so without any sign of regret, then it may not be clear to South that a squeeze has begun. He may decide to tackle the diamonds while still in hand.

A progressive squeeze is always a possibility when the opposing strength is known to be in one hand. This deal was unusual because of the criss-cross element:

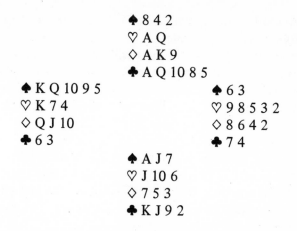

♠ 8 4 2
♡ A Q
♢ A K 9
♣ A Q 10 8 5

♠ K Q 10 9 5
♡ K 7 4
♢ Q J 10
♣ 6 3

♠ 6 3
♡ 9 8 5 3 2
♢ 8 6 4 2
♣ 7 4

♠ A J 7
♡ J 10 6
♢ 7 5 3
♣ K J 9 2

West, not vulnerable against vulnerable opponents, opened
One Spade, North doubled, and South responded 2 NT.
North carried him to 6 NT and West led the King of spades.
This was allowed to hold and West followed with the Queen
of diamonds. South came to hand with a club, finessed the
Queen of hearts, and led three more clubs, arriving at this
position:

♠ 8 4
♡ A
♢ K 9
♣ 10

♠ Q 10
♡ K 7
♢ J 10
♣ —

immaterial

♠ A J
♡ J 10
♢ 7 5
♣ —

When south cashed the last club, discarding a diamond
from hand, West was under the hammer. He may discard:

(a) A spade: South will cash ♡ A, a *Vienna Coup*, then follow with two spades.

(b) A heart; the Ace of hearts will now drop the King and South will follow with Ace of spades and Jack of hearts.

(c) A diamond; South follows with King and 9 of diamonds, discarding ♠ J, and West is trapped in a criss-cross squeeze.

Note that there is a defence to this contract if declarer plays off the Ace of hearts early on, hoping to drop a doubleton King. West can then throw a diamond on the last club and South will make an extra trick in diamonds, but West will then be discarding after the declarer.

The precise arrangement of menaces described so far in this chapter is comparatively rare. When two tricks are won by a squeeze, it is usually done with the aid of an extended menace. This type of progressive ending can be contained in four cards:

```
                    ♠ A J 10
                    ♡ —
                    ◇ —
                    ♣ J
                                    ♠ K Q
                                    ♡ J
       immaterial                   ◇ 10
                                    ♣ —
                    ♠ 4
                    ♡ 10
                    ◇ 9
                    ♣ K
```

When South plays off the King of clubs East must relinquish two tricks. A spade is immediately fatal, so he discards the Jack of hearts or the 10 of diamonds. South's established winner extracts a further tooth. The squeeze would work equally well against West. The opportunity for this sort of squeeze arises when there is a long suit in dummy and a possibility that the player who has a guard in this suit may also control two other suits.

♠ A 8
♡ 9 4 3
♢ A K 7 6 2
♣ Q 8 4

Contract: 4 ♡
Lead:　　♣ K

♠ Q 7
♡ A K Q J 2
♢ Q 3
♣ 10 7 5 3

South plays in Four Hearts after West has doubled the opening bid of One Heart. The defence begins with Ace, King and another club. East ruffs and returns the 10 of spades.

East would return a spade at this point even if he held the King, but nevertheless declarer must not part with the Queen of spades, because it is unlikely to win and may be useful later as a menace against West, who is known to hold the Jack of clubs.

The 10 of spades runs to the Ace, therefore, and South plays off two top hearts. Had the 10 fallen, declarer could have ruffed the fourth club, but in practice West discards on the second heart. There is a good chance now that West's responsibilities will include long diamonds and the controls in spades and clubs. The full deal is:

```
              ♠ A 8
              ♡ 9 4 3
              ◇ A K 7 6 2
              ♣ Q 8 4
♠ K J 6 5                      ♠ 10 9 4 3 2
♡ 8                           ♡ 10 7 6 5
◇ J 9 8 5                     ◇ 10 4
♣ A K J 9                     ♣ 6 2
              ♠ Q 7
              ♡ A K Q J 2
              ◇ Q 3
              ♣ 10 7 5 3
```

After three rounds of clubs and a spade to the Ace, South plays off all his trumps and West is crushed. The extended menace in diamonds compensates for the lack of a second two-card menace.

Strange things can happen when there are extended menaces in more than one suit. Consider this deal from match play:

```
              ♠ A 10 9 5
              ♡ 7 5
              ◇ 6 2
              ♣ A K J 8 5
♠ K J 7                       ♠ 8 6 4 3 2
♡ 3                           ♡ K 10 9 8 6 4 2
◇ Q 10 7 4                    ◇ —
♣ Q 10 9 7 3                  ♣ 6
              ♠ Q
              ♡ A Q J
              ◇ A K J 9 8 5 3
              ♣ 4 2
```

East elected to open Three Hearts and South ventured 3 NT. The bidding continued:

South	West	North	East
—	—	—	3♡
3 NT	No	4♣	No
4◊	No	4♠	No
4 NT	No	6 NT	No
No	dble	No	No
No			

West opened his singleton heart, East played the 8 and South won. Taking his time, South worked out that West, with at most ♠ K J and ♣ Q under the suits bid by North, must hold a double guard in diamonds, because at I.M.P. scoring players do not lightly double an opposing slam. In any case, it could cost nothing to make West discard on two more rounds of hearts. South crossed to ♣ K and finessed ♡ J, West discarding a club. This left:

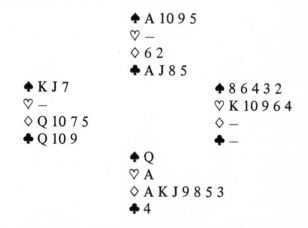

West was in bad trouble when the Ace of hearts was led. He cannot throw a diamond without allowing South to duck a diamond and run the rest of the suit. If West throws a club, South will run four tricks in this suit and end-play West in spades and diamonds. So West threw a spade. South now cashed the Ace of diamonds and followed with Ace and 5 of spades. West exited with the 10 of clubs, the Jack held, and West was squeezed again when the spades were cashed.

Counting the finesses in hearts and clubs, South had only nine tricks on top at the beginning of the play. However, he could always develop a tenth trick in spades, so the deal does not dispose of the tenet that a squeeze can never gain more than two tricks. But it was only by playing on hearts that the declarer could progress from nine tricks to twelve, and it is interesting that to play off a top diamond early on would spoil the communications.

9. Pressure in Space

In those desperate situations where to tackle any of the unestablished suits will achieve nothing, you may decide, quite rightly, to play off such winners as you possess in a fourth suit. It is surprising how often a defender will be forced to yield an advantage. The purpose of this chapter is to extend your appreciation of the variety of ways in which a man can feel the pinch.

Take this deal as a starting-point:

```
                    ♠ 6 4 2
                    ♡ K Q 7
                    ◊ A 5
                    ♣ A 8 5 4 2
Contract: 3 NT
Lead:     ♠ K
                    ♠ A 10 7
                    ♡ 4 3
                    ◊ K Q J 10 4
                    ♣ K 7 3
```

South plays in 3 NT after West has opened One Spade. West leads the King of spades. Since West is marked with the quick entry, the Ace of hearts, to hold up the Ace of spades is not important, except that by doing so you learn the division of the suit. So you hold up until the third round, on which east discards a heart.

Since West is marked with four spade winners and the Ace of hearts, what chance have you got? It would surprise some players to be told that all that was required was that West should hold three clubs. In that case, after three rounds of spades and four rounds of diamonds the position will be:

```
            ♠ —
            ♡ K Q 7
            ◇ —
            ♣ A 8 5
♠ J x
♡ A
◇ —                              immaterial
♣ Q x x
            ♠ —
            ♡ 4 3
            ◇ 10
            ♣ K 7 3
```

West has no good discard on the last diamond.

You may say that this is an ordinary squeeze-without-the-count. Not quite ordinary, however; three suits are involved and you have the special feature that West cannot let go a spade because in that case you will have time to develop a trick in hearts.

There are several combinations where a defender cannot lightly discard from an innocuous holding such as A x x. If you appreciate that, you will find the right line of play on this deal:

```
                    ♠ 9 6 5
                    ♡ K 7 2
                    ◇ A J 4
                    ♣ K Q 10 3
♠ Q J 10 4                          ♠ 8 7 2
♡ A 9 5                             ♡ J 10 8 3
◇ 8 6 5                             ◇ 10 9 3
♣ 8 6 4                             ♣ 9 5 2
                    ♠ A K 3
                    ♡ Q 6 4
                    ◇ K Q 7 2
                    ♣ A J 7
```

You play in 6 NT and West leads the Queen of spades. Looking at the North–South cards only, you may think that your only chance is to find a defender with a singleton or doubleton Ace of hearts. Not so; dummy's 9 of spades is a menace against West in all probability, and if West has the Ace of hearts the contract is cold!

Because you will want to be in your own hand to exert the pressure in hearts, you must play clubs before diamonds. This will be the position when the last diamond is led:

```
                        ♠ 9 6
                        ♡ K 7 2
                        ◇ —
                        ♣ —

     ♠ J 10
     ♡ A 9 5                              immaterial
     ◇ —
     ♣ —

                        ♠ K
                        ♡ Q 6 4
                        ◇ K
                        ♣ —
```

West can go home. If he throws a spade, dummy's ♠ 9 becomes good, and if he throws a heart dummy will discard a spade (not a heart, which would allow West to block the suit by going up with ♡ A on the next round).

A holding of A x x may become vulnerable even when under K Q x. Here the defenders appear to have succeeded with a forcing game:

```
                    ♠ K Q 6
                    ♡ A Q
                    ◇ A 10 4
                    ♣ 7 6 4 3 2
   ♠ A 8 4                        ♠ J 10 9 3
   ♡ K 7 3                        ♡ 10 9 6 4
   ◇ 8 3                          ◇ 7 6 5
   ♣ A K J 10 9                   ♣ 8 5
                    ♠ 7 5 2
                    ♡ J 8 5 2
                    ◇ K Q J 9 2
                    ♣ Q
```

With both sides vulnerable the bidding goes:

South	West	North	East
No	1♣	dble	No
2◇	No	3◇	No
3♡	No	5◇	No
No	No		

West holds the first trick with the King of clubs. A switch to a trump is worth considering, but west will probably lead a second club, forcing South to ruff. A finesse of ♡ Q stands up. South cashes the Ace of hearts, plays a diamond to the King and leads a third heart. When the King appears, he ruffs with ◇ A and draws trumps, arriving at this position:

```
            ♠ K Q 6
            ♡ —
            ◇ —
            ♣ 7 6
♠ A 8 6
♡ —                        immaterial
◇ —
♣ J 10
            ♠ 7 5 2
            ♡ J
            ◇ 9
            ♣ —
```

South has been short of entries for all he wants to do, but now West must come to his rescue. The Jack of hearts is led before the last trump – and before a spade. West's best chance is to throw a spade. Declarer then leads a spade to the King and plays a low spade from the table.

There is another time when a defender with A x x can ill spare a low card: this is when he needs to hold up the Ace to cut communications.

```
                ♠ A J 6 3
                ♡ A 5
                ◇ K Q J 10
                ♣ 7 5 3
♠ K Q 10 5                      ♠ 9 8 4 2
♡ 9 2                           ♡ 8 7 6 3
◇ A 4 3                         ◇ 9 7 2
♣ 10 9 6 2                      ♣ K 8
                ♠ 7
                ♡ K Q J 10 4
                ◇ 8 6 5
                ♣ A Q J 4
```

Playing in Six Hearts, South won the spade lead in dummy, finessed ♣ Q, crossed to ♡ A, and led a second club, on which the King appeared. All followed to the King of hearts. On the third round of trumps West discarded a spade, but the fourth round proved strangely embarrassing:

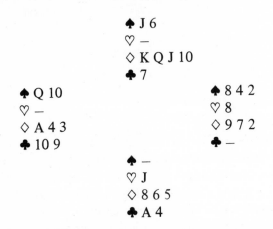

```
                    ♠ J 6
                    ♡ —
                    ◇ K Q J 10
                    ♣ 7
    ♠ Q 10                        ♠ 8 4 2
    ♡ —                           ♡ 8
    ◇ A 4 3                       ◇ 9 7 2
    ♣ 10 9                        ♣ —
                    ♠ —
                    ♡ J
                    ◇ 8 6 5
                    ♣ A 4
```

South had not been thinking about a squeeze at all, but when West went into a huddle the situation became clear. Obviously West could not part with a club, and if he threw a diamond he would not be able to hold up the Ace for two rounds. So in the end West threw a spade. South then discarded a *diamond* from dummy and used the two diamond entries to establish a spade winner.

Is there any other reason why a defender should need to keep low cards with an Ace or King? Well, if you hold A x or K x in a suit of which your partner holds the corresponding honour, you may wish to be able to keep in touch, may you not? Even this innocent desire can be exploited.

```
              ♠ Q 9
              ♡ A 9 8 7
              ◇ K Q 5 3
              ♣ J 10 4
♠ K J 8 4 2                    ♠ 10 5 3
♡ Q J 5 2                      ♡ 10 6 4
◇ 10 9                         ◇ 8 6 2
♣ A 3                          ♣ K 9 7 6
              ♠ A 7 6
              ♡ K 3
              ◇ A J 7 4
              ♣ Q 8 5 2
```

South played in 3 NT and West led a spade, won by
dummy's Queen. Against most opponents the 10 of clubs
from dummy would win the contract, but South was up
against strong opposition and knew that East, if possible,
would win with the Ace or King and clear the spades while
his partner still had an entry. Following a sound general
principle, South began with Ace, Jack and another diamond.

West showed signs of discomfort on the third round of
diamonds. You can see why. If he throws a spade he allows
declarer to set up a club trick, losing just two spades and two
clubs. A heart will cost a trick, evidently. And if he discards a
club from A x he deprives his partner of the chance to act the
hero on the first round of the suit. The best play for West, no
doubt, is to discard a heart without any sign of anxiety,
because South may not be able to read the position; but in
life players pause to think when they have a problem, and a
clever declarer always asks himself, 'What's he thinking about?'

Note that to play a club at trick two, and the diamonds
later, is not good enough: East goes up with ♣ K to clear the
spades, and when diamonds are led West must trust his partner
for the 10 of hearts.

This is one more hand where pressure in space forces a
defender to inconvenient discards in a suit of which he holds
the Ace:

```
              ♠ K 10 6 3
              ♡ Q J 8
              ◇ Q 7 4
              ♣ A 5 2
♠ 8                            ♠ A 9 7 5 2
♡ 9 4 2                        ♡ A 10 7 3
◇ J 10 6 3                     ◇ 9 5 2
♣ K Q J 10 6                   ♣ 9
              ♠ Q J 4
              ♡ K 6 5
              ◇ A K 8
              ♣ 8 7 4 3
```

South plays in 3 NT and the King of clubs is led. If only to discover how the suit is divided, South holds off for two rounds, winning the third. East, who can see that his long cards in hearts and spades may be a threat to the declarer, discards two diamonds.

As West has four club tricks, the contract can be made only if East holds both the major-suit Aces. After winning with ♣ A South plays Queen and Jack of spades. East holds off; he is ready to pounce on the third round and return the suit while he still holds the Ace of hearts. Declarer tries next to establish tricks in hearts, but again East holds off. The position is now:

```
              ♠ K 10
              ♡ Q 8
              ◇ Q 7 4
              ♣ —
♠ —                            ♠ A 9 7
♡ 9                            ♡ A 10 7
◇ J 10 6 3                     ◇ 9
♣ Q 6                          ♣ —
              ♠ 4
              ♡ K 5
              ◇ A K 8
              ♣ 7
```

Another round of either major suit would bring defeat, but observe the effect of playing Ace and King of diamonds: East must abandon his potential winner in one of the major suits and South at once plays on this suit.

The moral of this chapter is that you must do more than look for orthodox squeeze endings. There are innumerable occasions, often difficult to recognize in advance, where the play of a winning card quite early in the play will cause the defence to crumble.

10.   Exotica

Squeeze play has its gryphons: animals with a lion's body and an eagle's beak and wings. Notwithstanding some of our earlier pronouncements, there are squeeze positions in which there is no entry to one of the hands; in which there is no two-card menace; in which there is not even a menace in two suits; in which it is necessary to give up a trick to win two tricks; in which a combination as lowly as 5 2, with the Ace, King and Queen against it, can exercise a threat. In the course of this chapter we confirm the reality of all these oddities, though sometimes only with a miniature diagram, because they are too difficult or too infrequent to be of practical importance. We begin with a study of a squeeze that involves the element of finesse. This is the guard squeeze, neither rare nor difficult.

Guard squeeze

Everyone knows the situation where it is unsafe to unguard an honour because this would leave partner exposed to a finesse; the commonest example occurs when one defender holds Q x and his partner J x x. When the player who holds the shorter guard – the player with Q x – needs to protect two other suits, he may find his responsibilities too numerous.

```
            ♠ 8
            ♡ A 4
            ◇ 9
            ♣ —
♠ Q                         ♠ 5
♡ Q 3                       ♡ J 9 2
◇ 10                        ◇ —
♣ —                         ♣ —
            ♠ —
            ♡ K 10 5
            ◇ —
            ♣ Q
```

Playing notrumps, South leads the Queen of clubs. Obviously West cannot part with a diamond or a spade, and if he throws a heart he exposes his partner to a finesse.

Now we draw your attention to an important fact, common to all guard squeezes: the squeeze would be equally effective if East held, instead of the valueless ♠ 5, a master card in either spades or diamonds. Give East the 10 of spades instead of the ♠ 5, and we have:

```
            ♠ 8
            ♡ A 4
            ◇ 9
            ♣ —
♠ Q                         ♠ 10
♡ Q 3                       ♡ J 9 2
◇ 10                        ◇ —
♣ —                         ♣ —
            ♠ —
            ♡ K 10 5
            ◇ —
            ♣ Q
```

Now West, on the lead of ♣ Q, will be disposed to throw the Queen of spades. Dummy then discards ◊ 9, and East is squeezed. Since it involves both opponents, this is sometimes called a double guard squeeze, but the distinction is not really valid because, in the nature of things, a guard squeeze always involves both opponents. (It is possible to construct a genuine double guard squeeze, in which each opponent has to protect his partner from a finesse.)

A noticeable feature of the guard squeeze is that a single menace controlled by both opponents possesses value. This is very rare, occurring only in the guard squeeze and some complicated positions known as 'clash squeezes'.

Quite often, as in the next example, the declarer may need to unblock in the suit of the double-entry menace.

♠ A J 5 3
♡ K 9 4
◊ 8 7 2
♣ 10 7 4

Contract: 6 ♠
Lead: ♣ Q

♠ K Q 10 8 7 4 2
♡ A 8 3
◊ 6
♣ A K

You are in Six Spades and West leads the Queen of clubs. You have eleven tricks on top and the twelfth can come only from a squeeze. Your first thought may be: 'Obviously I have a menace against West in clubs; if I can find him with control in hearts – any five hearts – I can squeeze him after giving up a diamond'.

True enough, but there is another substantial chance. If West has any two heart honours, and the defenders do not attack hearts when they come in, the contract cannot fail! Suppose this to be the full hand:

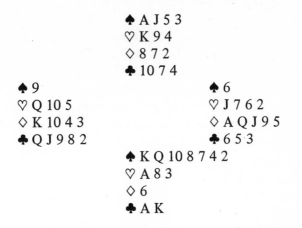

♠ A J 5 3
♡ K 9 4
♢ 8 7 2
♣ 10 7 4

♠ 9
♡ Q 10 5
♢ K 10 4 3
♣ Q J 9 8 2

♠ 6
♡ J 7 6 2
♢ A Q J 9 5
♣ 6 5 3

♠ K Q 10 8 7 4 2
♡ A 8 3
♢ 6
♣ A K

Having won the first trick with ♣ A, you draw a round of trumps, then lead a low diamond from the table. East plays the Ace, and it is most unlikely now that he will find the switch to hearts. Probably he will lead a second club. You then advance towards this ending:

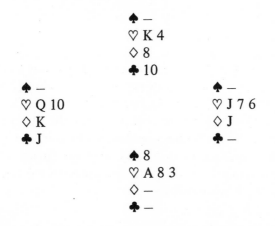

♠ —
♡ K 4
♢ 8
♣ 10

♠ —
♡ Q 10
♢ K
♣ J

♠ —
♡ J 7 6
♢ J
♣ —

♠ 8
♡ A 8 3
♢ —
♣ —

Note that you have unblocked ♡ 9, a necessary measure, and that you have retained a diamond in dummy. On the last spade an inexpert West would throw a diamond, knowing that his partner had a control in this suit; but then dummy would throw a club and East would be squeezed, whatever his heart holding. It is better play for West to discard ♡ 10; this would be good enough if East's hearts were J 8 x, but as the cards lie East is exposed to a finesse.

There is another type of guard squeeze, less common and more difficult, so we will deal with it briefly, showing just the end-position:

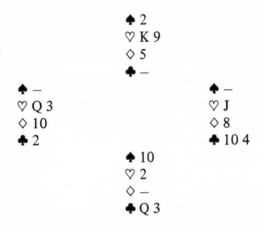

South leads the 10 of spades and West discards a club. As before, East has responsibilities in three suits; he may discard a diamond for the moment, but then the Queen of clubs will squeeze West. Note, once again, that the diamond 5 is valuable even though both opponents can beat it, and another point is that South must not begin with the Queen of clubs, discarding a spade from dummy, because then North will be squeezed before East on the next trick.

The winkle*

We remarked at the beginning of this chapter that so lowly a holding as 5 2 could exert a threat even when opponents

*First so named by Terence Reese in *The Expert Game*.

held Ace, King and Queen, not all in the same hand. If you were doubtful, examine this diagram:

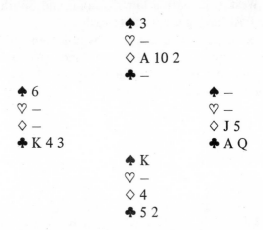

```
              ♠ 3
              ♡ —
              ◇ A 10 2
              ♣ —
♠ 6                        ♠ —
♡ —                        ♡ —
◇ —                        ◇ J 5
♣ K 4 3                    ♣ A Q
              ♠ K
              ♡ —
              ◇ 4
              ♣ 5 2
```

Needing three of the last four tricks, South cashes the King of spades. What is East to throw? If the Queen of clubs, he is thrown in on the next trick, so he attempts to avoid this by discarding the Ace of clubs. Now South leads the 2 of clubs and West is embarrassed. This was a fancy ending, but it shows the power of the winkle squeeze, which sometimes occurs in quite a natural setting:

```
              ♠ 6 4
              ♡ 9 6 4 3 2
              ◇ 10 5
              ♣ A K 6 4
♠ 9 8 7 3                  ♠ 5 2
♡ 5                        ♡ A Q J 8
◇ J 8 6 4 2                ◇ K Q 7
♣ 8 5 3                    ♣ J 10 9 2
              ♠ A K Q J 10
              ♡ K 10 7
              ◇ A 9 3
              ♣ Q 7
```

South plays in Four Spades. East wins the first trick with the Ace of hearts and returns the Queen, which is covered and ruffed. West exits with a low diamond and South must win, because East has a good heart to cash.

Prospects seem poor, because there is not even the threat of a throw-in, forcing a lead into a tenace. Nevertheless, declarer can winkle a trick from the diamonds. He plays four rounds of trumps, reaching this position:

```
                    ♠ —
                    ♡ 9
                    ◇ 10
                    ♣ A K 6 4
    ♠ —                         ♠ —
    ♡ —                         ♡ J
    ◇ J 8 6                     ◇ K
    ♣ 8 5 3                     ♣ J 10 9 2
                    ♠ J
                    ♡ 10
                    ◇ 9 3
                    ♣ Q 7
```

On the Jack of spades a heart is thrown from dummy and East has no good discard. He must throw a diamond, but South will then establish a trick for ◇ 9.

Finally, a winkle may produce a surprise trick when there is a blocked suit:

```
                    ♠ 10 6 2
                    ♡ A 7 4
                    ◇ A J 6 5
                    ♣ 9 4 2
    ♠ J 8 7 4                   ♠ 9 5 3
    ♡ Q J 10                    ♡ K 8 6 2
    ◇ Q 10 7                    ◇ 9 8 4 3 2
    ♣ J 6 3                     ♣ 8
                    ♠ A K Q
                    ♡ 9 5 3
                    ◇ K
                    ♣ A K Q 10 7 5
```

South is in Six Clubs and West leads the Queen of hearts. This is annoying, because now the diamonds are blocked. The way the hand will go cannot be foreseen with any certainty, but the defence will be more difficult if South wins than if he holds off, so he plays ♡ A at trick one and leads two rounds of trumps. When the Jack does not drop, he plays off clubs and spades, arriving at this position:

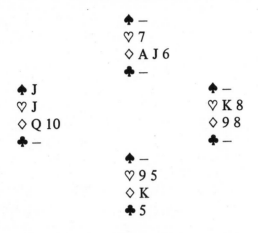

The defenders have made the best discards, but what is West to throw on the last club? If a spade, South will cash ◇ K and exit with a low heart. If the Jack of hearts, dummy will throw a diamond and now East will be in difficulties. When East throws a diamond, South will overtake the King of diamonds and lead a heart from dummy, winkling a trick for the 9 of hearts.

A squeeze of this type is not easy to plan in detail, but if you are aware of the possibilities you will at least not hesitate to put opponents under pressure by playing off all your immediate winners.

Entry squeeze

The last deal possessed in one variation the characteristics of the entry squeeze, which is our next subject. Many types

of ending can be included under this heading. This is a
'stepping-stone' squeeze, quite common at the table:

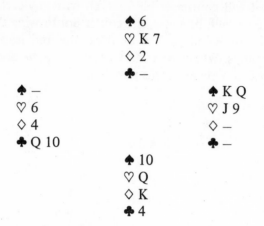

```
              ♠ 6
              ♡ K 7
              ◇ 2
              ♣ —
♠ —                        ♠ K Q
♡ 6                        ♡ J 9
◇ 4                        ◇ —
♣ Q 10                     ♣ —
              ♠ 10
              ♡ Q
              ◇ K
              ♣ 4
```

There is a block in hearts, but the situation is restored
when South leads the King of diamonds. East must throw a
spade. South then cashes the Queen of hearts and exits with
a spade, using East as a stepping-stone to the heart winner in
dummy.

You may consider that the next diagram illustrates a no-
entry rather than an entry squeeze:

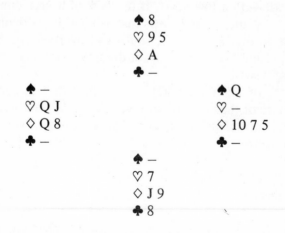

```
              ♠ 8
              ♡ 9 5
              ◇ A
              ♣ —
♠ —                        ♠ Q
♡ Q J                      ♡ —
◇ Q 8                      ◇ 10 7 5
♣ —                        ♣ —
              ♠ —
              ♡ 7
              ◇ J 9
              ♣ 8
```

South needs three of the last four tricks, and there doesn't seem to be much he can do about it, because after he has cashed the club winner he is apparently cut off from his own hand. But the defenders have their problems, too. West cannot let go a heart on ♣ 8, as this will enable South to establish a winner in dummy, so he must discard the 8 of diamonds. South then leads a diamond to the Ace, bringing down the Queen, and exits with a spade from the table in a stepping-stone position. The ending arose from the following deal:

```
                    ♠ 8 6 4 2
                    ♡ A 9 5 3
                    ◊ A K
                    ♣ K Q J
     ♠ 9 7                           ♠ Q 10 5 3
     ♡ K Q J 8 4 2                   ♡ 10
     ◊ Q 8 4 3                       ◊ 10 7 6 5
     ♣ 6                             ♣ 10 9 5 4
                    ♠ A K J
                    ♡ 7 6
                    ◊ J 9 2
                    ♣ A 8 7 3 2
```

South played in Six Clubs after West had overcalled in hearts. Because of the danger of a ruff, South had to win the heart lead. When West showed out on the second round of trumps, it became impractical to ruff a diamond. Declarer cashed a third club, crossed to ♠ A, and drew the outstanding trump. After a diamond to the King he finessed ♠ J and cashed the King, to arrive at the position shown in the first diagram.

Jettison squeeze

Not far removed from the entry squeeze is the jettison squeeze, where a winner is discarded on the squeeze card. These situations arise when there is a problem with entries.

```
            ♠ A K 6 4
            ♡ 7 3
            ◇ 7 5 3 2
            ♣ A K Q
♠ J 9 2                    ♠ Q 10 8 7
♡ 6 2                      ♡ 9 8 5 4
◇ A K 10 8                 ◇ Q J 9
♣ 9 7 4 2                  ♣ 10 8
            ♠ 5 3
            ♡ A K Q J 10
            ◇ 6 4
            ♣ J 6 5 3
```

At some tables in a pairs contest the bidding went:

South	North
—	1♣
1♡	1♠
3♡	4♡
No	

West leads the King of diamonds against Four Spades and South has to ruff the third round. Ten tricks are reasonably safe, but in a pairs it is legitimate to take a slight risk by cashing the top spades and precisely two top clubs before running the hearts. (If clubs are 3–3, nothing is lost because dummy's high club can if necessary be discarded on the last trump.) This line of play produces an extra trick, because after three rounds of trumps the position is:

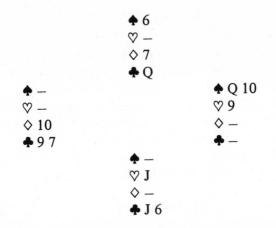

<pre>
            ♠ 6
            ♡ —
            ◇ 7
            ♣ Q
♠ —   ♠ Q 10
♡ —   ♡ 9
◇ 10   ◇ —
♣ 9 7   ♣ —
            ♠ —
            ♡ J
            ◇ —
            ♣ J 6
</pre>

When the last heart is led, West cannot spare the master diamond, so he throws a club. Keeping his head, South jettisons ♣ Q from dummy and makes an overtrick.

Many problems can be built around the jettison squeeze. In some the declarer discards a winner from dummy to set up a one-card menace in his own hand, leading to a progressive squeeze worth two tricks. In a full deal of thirteen cards it is generally possible to arrange matters more simply.

Overtaking squeeze

The alternative description, see-saw squeeze, well describes the manoeuvre on the following deal:

<pre>
                ♠ A Q 5 3 2
                ♡ Q 8
                ◇ 5
                ♣ J 8 6 4 3
♠ 9   ♠ 8 7
♡ 4 2   ♡ J 10 9 7 6 5 3
◇ K Q 10 6 4   ◇ J 2
♣ K Q 10 5 2   ♣ 9 7
                ♠ K J 10 6 4
                ♡ A K
                ◇ A 9 8 7 3
                ♣ A
</pre>

South opens One Spade and West, in the manner of so many players, overcalls with the tell-tale 2 NT, denoting length in both minors. North raises to Four Spades, and after discovering that his partner holds second-round control of diamonds South battles his way to Seven Spades.

The King of diamonds is led and South realizes that he cannot conveniently take four ruffs in either hand. However, he can exploit his knowledge of West's two-suiter by taking one round of trumps, cashing the top hearts and the Ace of clubs, and leading the King of spades at this point:

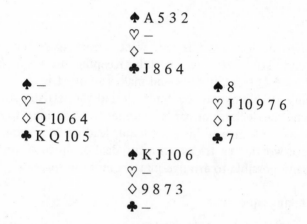

```
              ♠ A 5 3 2
              ♡ —
              ♢ —
              ♣ J 8 6 4
♠ —                          ♠ 8
♡ —                          ♡ J 10 9 7 6
♢ Q 10 6 4                   ♢ J
♣ K Q 10 5                   ♣ 7
              ♠ K J 10 6
              ♡ —
              ♢ 9 8 7 3
              ♣ —
```

West is now uncomfortably perched on the see-saw. If West discards a diamond, South will play low from dummy and establish a diamond winner, and if West discards a club South will overtake the spade King and set up a trick in clubs.

Double trump squeeze

Quite often in bridge articles, though not very often at the table, declarer will have a chance to bring off a trump squeeze that involves both opponents.

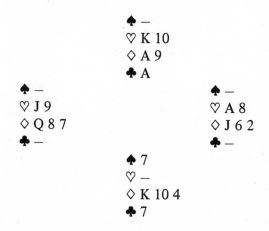

                 ♠ K 6 4 2
                 ♡ K 10 5
                 ◇ A 9 3
                 ♣ A Q J

♠ 10   ♠ 8 3
♡ Q J 9 4   ♡ A 8 7 3 2
◇ Q 8 7 5   ◇ J 6 2
♣ 10 6 4 2   ♣ 9 8 5

                 ♠ A Q J 9 7 5
                 ♡ 6
                 ◇ K 10 4
                 ♣ K 7 3

South is in Six Spades and West leads the Queen of hearts. South plays low from dummy, maintaining a twin threat, and West wisely switches to a club. After five rounds of spades and a second round of clubs the position is:

                 ♠ —
                 ♡ K 10
                 ◇ A 9
                 ♣ A

♠ —   ♠ —
♡ J 9   ♡ A 8
◇ Q 8 7   ◇ J 6 2
♣ —   ♣ —

                 ♠ 7
                 ♡ —
                 ◇ K 10 4
                 ♣ 7

On the next club neither defender can throw a heart without allowing South to develop a trick in this suit; and if both discard a diamond, they fare no better.

Three-suit trump squeeze

There is a little known, but by no means useless, variation of the ruffing squeeze, in which the declarer profits from the presence of two one-card menaces in the opposite hand, even though both are controlled by the opponent who sits over them.


```
                      ♠ J 7 4
                      ♡ 8 6 5 2
                      ◇ K 4
                      ♣ A 9 6 2
      ♠ 9 8 6 5 3                      ♠ K Q 10 2
      ♡ Q 9 4                          ♡ A K J 10
      ◇ 7                              ◇ 6 2
      ♣ 10 8 7 3                       ♣ K J 5
                      ♠ A
                      ♡ 7 3
                      ◇ A Q J 10 9 8 5 3
                      ♣ Q 4
```

At game all the bidding goes:

South	West	North	East
—	—	No	1♡
3◇	No	4◇	No
5◇	No	No	No

West leads the 4 of hearts and after making two heart tricks East switches to the King of spades.

Since evidently East has the control of both major suits, South cannot hope to develop a squeeze against West, so he must aim to embarrass East, who may hold the King of clubs. After Ace of diamonds and a diamond to the King declarer ruffs the third round of hearts, to isolate the menace, and runs off trumps, arriving at this position:

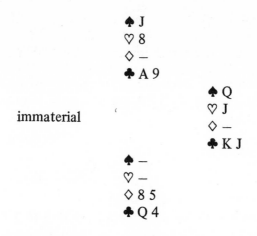

```
            ♠ J
            ♡ 8
            ◇ —
            ♣ A 9
                        ♠ Q
                        ♡ J
  immaterial            ◇ —
                        ♣ K J
            ♠ —
            ♡ —
            ◇ 8 5
            ♣ Q 4
```

On the 8 of diamonds a club is thrown from dummy and East must abandon one of his charges.

One-suit squeeze

Every squeeze has a menace in two suits – or does it? It is a question of semantics, perhaps, but there is undoubtedly an element of pressure in this type of ending, which is not so uncommon:

```
                ♠ 7 5 3
                ♡ —
                ◇ Q
                ♣ —
  ♠ K J 10 6                ♠ 9 4
  ♡ —                       ♡ J
  ◇ —                       ◇ —
  ♣ —                       ♣ 5
                ♠ A Q 8
                ♡ —
                ◇ 10
                ♣ —
```

Diamonds are trumps, the lead is in dummy, and South can afford to lose only one trick. Most declarers would lead a low spade from dummy, hoping to duck the trick into West's hand, but this plan is frustrated if East is sufficiently awake to insert the 9. Try, instead, the effect of leading the last trump. There is then no defence, whether or not West attempts to unblock.

Backwash squeeze

Ah yes, we said at the beginning of this chapter that a squeeze was possible even when there was no two-card menace in either hand. This is the ending that justifies that statement:

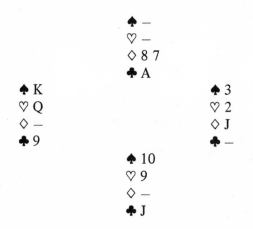

♠ —
♡ —
♢ 8 7
♣ A

♠ K   ♠ 3
♡ Q   ♡ 2
♢ —   ♢ J
♣ 9   ♣ —

♠ 10
♡ 9
♢ —
♣ J

Clubs are trumps and the lead is in dummy. It looks as though South, after establishing a diamond winner by ruffing, will not be able to enter dummy to draw the outstanding trump. But West is strangely embarrassed when ♢ 7 is ruffed by ♣ J. If West underruffs, dummy's last two cards are high, and if he throws a spade or a heart South will follow with a newly established winner in that suit.

This has not been in any way a comprehensive account of irregular squeezes. There are many other types, mostly too rare and too complicated to be of importance for practical play.

11. Defence to Squeeze Play

Defending against a squeeze is a problem in two parts: finding the best discard when the threat is upon you, and taking precautionary measures to prevent the declarer from developing a genuine squeeze.

Principles of discarding

Although bridge writers seldom attach their minds to the subject, correct discarding when declarer leads a long suit is the most difficult part of the game. At the higher levels of play it leads to the longest 'trances'. Signalling must be well organized and the defenders must work hard to form a picture of the declarer's hand. Even when that has been done, the defence against a possible, but in fact imperfect, squeeze will be difficult unless certain principles are understood. Depending on the early defence, three different situations may arise from the following deal:

```
                    ♠ Q 7 3
                    ♡ A 7 4 2
                    ◇ K 6
                    ♣ A 8 5 3
  ♠ A K J 8 2                    ♠ 10 9 6 5
  ♡ J 10 5                       ♡ Q 9 8
  ◇ 8                            ◇ 7 4
  ♣ Q J 9 6                      ♣ K 10 4 2
                    ♠ 4
                    ♡ K 6 3
                    ◇ A Q J 10 9 5 3 2
                    ♣ 7
```

South plays in Six Diamonds and West holds the first trick with the King of spades. On this trick it is good play for East to signal, not mingily with the 6, but with the 9, to establish that he has an even number. In any case, West's most likely switch at trick two is to the Queen of clubs.

If South knows his onions he will attempt to isolate the menace in clubs by ruffing the second and third rounds. As the cards lie, nothing is gained. After five rounds of trumps the position is:

```
                    ♠ Q
                    ♡ A 7 4
                    ◇ —
                    ♣ 8
     ♠ A                        ♠ 10
     ♡ J 10 5                   ♡ Q 9 8
     ◇ —                        ◇ —
     ♣ J                        ♣ K
                    ♠ —
                    ♡ K 6 3
                    ◇ 5 3
                    ♣ —
```

When the next diamond is led, all of West's cards have a busy appearance. Knowing that his partner still has a club control, West may be tempted to part with the Jack of clubs. But this is fatal. On the last trump West must discard a heart and East is squeezed.

There are two reasons why West should know that he must discard a heart, not a club, on the penultimate trump. One is that he will certainly have to throw a heart on the last trump, so he may as well do this now. The second, more technical, reason is that a player who needs only to guard two one-card menaces can never feel the pinch. (It is true that in the present case the 10 of hearts might be a valuable card; but unless partner's hearts are as good as Q 9 x there will be no defence against the guard squeeze.

The situation shown in the diagram above is quite common: both defenders control the double-entry menace (hearts) and both control the single menace (clubs). In these circumstances the task of guarding the double menace should be left to the player who has no responsibilities in the third suit (spades).

Return now to the original deal and imagine that West switches to a *heart* at trick two. Suppose, first, that declarer wins with the Ace in dummy and runs the trumps, arriving at this position:

```
                    ♠ Q
                    ♡ 7 4
                    ◊ —
                    ♣ A 8
      ♠ A                        ♠ —
      ♡ 10 5                     ♡ Q 8
      ◊ —                        ◊ —
      ♣ Q J                      ♣ K 5 2
                    ♠ —
                    ♡ K 6
                    ◊ 5 3
                    ♣ 7
```

What is West to throw on the next trump? This time, if he throws a heart he gives declarer his chance. South discards a heart from dummy, cashes the King, and leads the last trump; it is the classic double squeeze ending, with clubs as the pivot suit.

However, a club from West in the diagram position defeats the squeeze. For the moment South discards a heart from dummy, but when he leads the last trump, West throwing another club, he has to make a premature discard from dummy. To throw a heart spoils the communications and if he throws the Queen of spades then East can spare a heart, leaving his partner to control this suit.

In this example there were two double menaces controlled by both opponents, and West in addition controlled a one-card menace. The principle he must follow is this: unguard the suit that is held on the left (clubs); retain a guard in the suit where the two-card menace is on the right (hearts). This is logical, because it is preferable to sit *over* a menace (South's second heart) rather than *under* a menace (North's second club).

The same principle would assist West if South were to win the heart switch in his own hand with the King. Then West would be under pressure quite early:

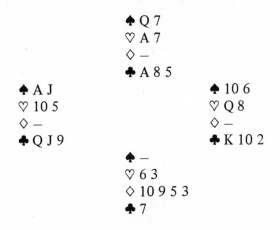

West must throw a club now, and another club on the next diamond. If he parts with a heart, leaving South with a menace card over East, there will be a double squeeze (heart to the Ace, spade ruff, last trump).

Sometimes a player who holds a poor hand will fail to protect his partner from a squeeze. The *locus classicus* for a misfortune of this kind is this deal from a match between England and Scotland:

♠ K J 9 4
♡ A 9
♢ J 10 5
♣ Q 9 7 6

♠ 8 3 2   ♠ Q 10 7 6 5
♡ 8 7 5 3   ♡ 2
♢ K 8 7 6   ♢ Q 4
♣ 4 3   ♣ K J 10 8 5

♠ A
♡ K Q J 10 6 4
♢ A 9 3 2
♣ A 2

With neither side vulnerable the bidding went:

South	West	North	East
–	–	1 NT (1)	2◊ (2)
6♡	No	No	No

(1) Intrepid.
(2) Astro, indicating spades and a minor suit.

West led a spade. Declarer crossed to the Ace of hearts
and correctly led a low diamond (East might have held a
singleton honour) to the 9 and King. West led a second round
of trumps; this was good play, because otherwise declarer
can negotiate a ruff of the fourth round of diamonds. South
won the trump lead in dummy and led the 10 of diamonds,
which was covered by the Queen and Ace. After three more
rounds of trumps the position was:

```
                    ♠ K J
                    ♡ —
                    ◊ 10
                    ♣ Q 9
    ♠ 3                              ♠ Q 10
    ♡ —                              ♡ —
    ◊ 8 7                            ◊ —
    ♣ 4 3                            ♣ K J 10
                    ♠ —
                    ♡ 4
                    ◊ 3 2
                    ♣ A 2
```

When the last heart was led, West knew he must keep his
diamonds and did not perceive that his nugatory holding in
the black suits possessed any value. He parted with a club,
and so did the others. Then a diamond to the 10 brought a
cry of anguish from East.

A defender who holds a guard in three suits will often be
pressed to find a discard that will present the declarer with
just one extra trick, and not two tricks. Such a situation
arose on this deal:

```
                    ♠ A Q 5
                    ♡ J 4 2
                    ◊ Q 6
                    ♣ Q J 10 7 4
    ♠ 9 4                              ♠ J 10 8 2
    ♡ 10 9 8 3                         ♡ Q 7 6 5
    ◊ J 9 2                            ◊ K 8 4
    ♣ K 8 6 2                          ♣ 9 3
                    ♠ K 7 6 3
                    ♡ A K
                    ◊ A 10 7 5 3
                    ♣ A 5
```

This was the bidding:

South	West	North	East
1◊	No	2♣	No
2♠	No	3♡ (1)	No
3 NT	No	4 NT (2)	No
No (3)	No	No	No

(1) Fourth suit, asking for further description.
(2) Natural, since no suit had been agreed.
(3) Well judged because, while South had the values for his reverse, the general texture of his hand was not promising for a slam.

West's lead of the 10 of hearts ran to the Ace and South played Ace and another club. West won the third round and led another heart. South crossed to the Queen of spades and East was under considerable pressure when the fifth club was led:

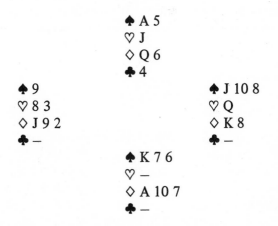

```
            ♠ A 5
            ♡ J
            ◊ Q 6
            ♣ 4
♠ 9                      ♠ J 10 8
♡ 8 3                    ♡ Q
◊ J 9 2                  ◊ K 8
♣ —                      ♣ —
            ♠ K 7 6
            ♡ —
            ◊ A 10 7
            ♣ —
```

It is clear that if East throws a heart or a diamond he can be subjected to a further squeeze, presenting declarer with two overtricks in his contract of 4 NT. In this type of position a player must unguard the suit held on his left. So long as East throws a spade he cannot be squeezed again.

Finally, there are occasions – not common, it is true – when a defender can save himself by 'discarding' a trump.

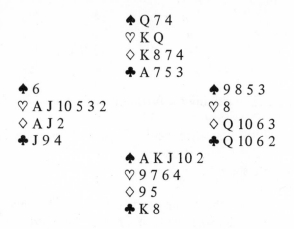

```
                    ♠ Q 7 4
                    ♡ K Q
                    ◇ K 8 7 4
                    ♣ A 7 5 3
    ♠ 6                         ♠ 9 8 5 3
    ♡ A J 10 5 3 2             ♡ 8
    ◇ A J 2                   ◇ Q 10 6 3
    ♣ J 9 4                   ♣ Q 10 6 2
                    ♠ A K J 10 2
                    ♡ 9 7 6 4
                    ◇ 9 5
                    ♣ K 8
```

South was in Four Spades and West began with Ace and another heart. East ruffed and put his partner in with the Ace of diamonds for another heart lead. Declarer ruffed high and East had to find a discard. It is easy to see that if East discards a diamond or a club he allows declarer to ruff out the suit and establish a winner. The only defence is to under-ruff. East cannot be squeezed later because both his menaces are on the right side of those in dummy.

It may be helpful to summarize the principles that we have noted in this section:

When there is a double-entry menace controlled by both defenders and a single menace controlled by both defenders, plus a single menace controlled by one defender, the player who has fewer suits to guard must be the one to retain control of the double-entry suit.

When there are two double menaces controlled by both defenders, and one defender in addition controls a one-card menace, this player must unguard the suit held on his left.

When a defender holds control of three suits and a progressive squeeze is threatened, this player's best chance (if the progressive squeeze is imperfect) will be to surrender a trick in the suit held on his left.

When a defender controls menaces in two suits where the length is held on his right, he may be able to escape destruction by underruffing in a suit that has been ruffed high in dummy.

Measures to avert a perfect squeeze

The props that underpin the structure of squeeze play are all subject to assault. The declarer, as we noted in earlier chapters, needs a fixed arrangement of menaces, timing, and entries. More often than not, the defenders will have a chance at some point in the play to disturb those arrangements.

To develop skill in this field, the first necessity is to be thoroughly practised in the technique of squeeze play from the declarer's side. It is the ex-poacher, after all, who makes the best gamekeeper. A reader to whom the contents of this book are comparatively new must not expect immediately to find far-sighted plays to defeat an opponent's squeeze. For the remainder of this chapter we will deal with the subject on as basic a level as possible.

The assault on menaces

The easiest way to defeat an impending squeeze is to destroy menaces, either by snuffing them out or by not allowing them to develop.

```
                        ♠ Q 6 5
                        ♡ A 8 7 4
                        ◇ J 7 5 3
                        ♣ 10 2
        ♠ A 4                           ♠ 9 7
        ♡ K J 3                         ♡ 10 9 5 2
        ◇ A K Q 8 6                     ◇ 9 2
        ♣ 9 8 3                         ♣ Q J 7 5 4
                        ♠ K J 10 8 3 2
                        ♡ Q 6
                        ◇ 10 4
                        ♣ A K 6
```

South plays in Four Spades after West has doubled the opening bid. West begins with two top diamonds. What next? He *must* kill the diamond menace in dummy. Since he posesses the Ace of trumps he knows he can do this effectively. At trick three he leads a low diamond for his partner to ruff, and when he comes in with the Ace of spades he extinguishes the diamond threat by leading a fourth round.

It is not difficult to see that if West defends in any other way South will develop a one-way squeeze. His last three cards will be ♡ Q 6 and ♠ 10, while dummy will hold ♡ A 8 and ◇ J.

The type of defence shown in the next example is more tricky. These are the hands of North and West:

```
                    ♠ 9 8 5 3
                    ♡ 10 4
                    ◇ A 7 5 2
                    ♣ A 6 3
        ♠ A K Q 10 6    N
        ♡ J 6
        ◇ K J 4      W       E
        ♣ 10 5 2         S
```

South, who has shown a powerful hand with long hearts, plays in Six Hearts after West has overcalled in spades. West leads the King of spades, on which his partner plays the 2 and declarer the 7. Most players, though not expecting to win the trick, would follow with a second round of spades. This mindless continuation of a 'safe' suit costs innumerable tricks. Often it helps the declarer to prepare for an elimination ending. Sometimes it enables him to shorten his trumps and develop an end-play in the trump suit, and sometimes, as here, it enables him to isolate a menace in preparation for a squeeze. This is the full hand:

```
                    ♠ 9 8 5 3
                    ♡ 10 4
                    ◇ A 7 5 2
                    ♣ A 6 3
        ♠ A K Q 10 6            ♠ J 4 2
        ♡ J 6                   ♡ 7 3
        ◇ K J 4                 ◇ 9 8 6 3
        ♣ 10 5 2                ♣ J 8 7 4
                    ♠ 7
                    ♡ A K Q 9 8 5 2
                    ◇ Q 10
                    ♣ K Q 9
```

South will ruff the second spade, draw trumps, cross to
Ace of clubs, and ruff a third spade, isolating the menace.
Then he will run off his winners in clubs and hearts, to West's
discomfiture.

The only winning defence at trick two is a club. A diamond
is an unnecessary risk and a heart gives dummy the vital extra
entry. If West makes the neutral lead of a club, then East's
Jack of spades will take the strain off West in the end-game.

The assault on timing

The essence of timing in any squeeze position is that the
defender should not have any idle cards. We have observed
such stratagems as the submarine squeeze, where the declarer
works to bring this situation about. In many cases the
defenders can counter by refusing to cash winners. Most
players have suffered at the table from partners who force
them to uncomfortable discards. It is perhaps more difficult
to recognize positions where a player may dig his own grave
by cashing one winner too many. This hand is typical:

```
                    ♠ J 7 5
                    ♡ A 5 3
                    ◇ A 6 4 2
                    ♣ A J 8
    ♠ K 10 8 6                     ♠ A 4 2
    ♡ Q J 9                        ♡ 7 6 4 2
    ◇ J 10 7 3                     ◇ 8
    ♣ 6 5                          ♣ K 9 7 3 2
                    ♠ Q 9 3
                    ♡ K 10 8
                    ◇ K Q 9 5
                    ♣ Q 10 4
```

South is in 3 NT. West leads a spade to his partner's Ace
and ducks the next round, letting South win with the Queen.
East wins the first round of clubs and fires back a spade.

Now the one thing West must not do is cash the thirteenth
spade. He has responsibilities in both red suits, and if he
cannot win a trick in one of those suits it will not avail him
to make the extra trick in spades. Generally speaking, it is
unwise for defenders to make their 'book' (four tricks when
defending against 3 NT) unless they have some idea where
the setting trick will come from.

If West cashes the spade winner he will be squeezed when
the next club is led. Instead, after making the King of spades
he must exit with his second club. Now, on the third club,
he must throw his spade winner. The best the declarer can
do, as the cards lie, is to play three rounds of hearts. West
wins and exits with the Jack or 10 of diamonds. So long as
partner holds the 8 or 9 of diamonds, West can prevent declarer
from making four tricks in the suit.

So far as possible, the defenders in a notrump contract
should keep their tricks on a loose rein. The meaning of that
observation will appear in this instructive deal:

```
                    ♠ K J 10 9
                    ♡ K 8
                    ◇ 10 6 4
                    ♣ A K J 4
♠ Q 3                                    ♠ A 7 4 2
♡ J 9 4 2                                ♡ 7 6 5
◇ Q J 9 8 3                              ◇ A 7 5
♣ 10 5                                   ♣ 9 6 2
                    ♠ 8 6 5
                    ♡ A Q 10 3
                    ◇ K 2
                    ♣ Q 8 7 3
```

South played in 3 NT and West led the Queen of diamonds. East overtook with the Ace and returned the 7 to South's King.

Four rounds of clubs now proved embarrassing for West. Knowing that South held four hearts, he decided in the end to part with his two spades. Reading the position well, South played Ace of hearts, a heart to the King, and then the 10 of diamonds from dummy. After running his diamond winners West was compelled to lead a heart into the declarer's Q 10. The Ace of spades withered on the vine.

What could the defence have done? The answer is that East made a tactical error in playing the Ace of diamonds on the opening lead. With an extra card in all the hands, the defence can withstand the pressure of the club leads. West lets go two spades, as before, but he is still in touch with his partner. When East comes in with the Ace of diamonds he cashes the Ace of spades. Many contracts can be saved by this type of defence.

Quite often it is a mistake for a defender to take a winner even when he knows he will never be in the lead again. We will illustrate this position with a miniature diagram:

```
              ♠ 6 2
              ♡ K 8 5
              ◇ A 4
              ♣ —
♠ 7                         ♠ K J 10
♡ Q 10 4                    ♡ 6 3
◇ Q J 3                     ◇ 9 2
♣ —                         ♣ —
              ♠ Q 5
              ♡ A 7
              ◇ K 8 6
              ♣ —
```

There are seven cards left and declarer has four top tricks.
He knows he can develop a trick in spades and leads low from
the table towards his Q 5. If East takes the King it will be the
last trick for the defence, because West will be squeezed on
the next round of spades. East must duck, and declarer will
then be unable to develop an extra trick.

That ingenious book *Right Through the Pack* contained an
amusing example of this idea. The distribution of the suit led
was something like this:

```
              ◇ A Q J
◇ 2                         ◇ K 10 9 8 7 6 5
              ◇ 4 3
```

When the Queen was finessed at trick one East had to duck.
West, who had one idle card, was able to discard safely on
the Ace of diamonds. If East had won the first trick the third
round of diamonds would have been a killer for his partner.
Essentially, plays of this kind deprive opponents of the use
of an effective squeeze card.

The assault on entries

While the assault on menace cards is the easiest way to
defeat a squeeze, and the assault on timing the most difficult,
the assault on entries is the most frequent. Sometimes it is

easy – just a matter of attacking in time the suit of the two-card menace. Sometimes the play is both difficult and risky. Most squeezes that depend on a double-entry menace can be defeated by an early lead of this suit, often from a dangerous holding such as J x x or Q x x.

This is a fairly simple example of the attack on a suit where the declarer has a divided menace:

```
                ♠ A 9 4 2
                ♡ K Q 5
                ◇ 7 3
                ♣ Q 8 5 2
♠ K 10 5                        ♠ J 8 6 3
♡ 10 9 8 4                      ♡ J 6 2
◇ 8                             ◇ Q J 10
♣ A K J 7 3                     ♣ 9 6 4
                ♠ Q 7
                ♡ A 7 3
                ◇ A K 9 6 5 4 2
                ♣ 10
```

Defending against Five Diamonds, West leads the King of clubs and switches to a heart. South wins and plays off Ace, King and another diamond. When he wins the third round East must not inertly return a club or a heart: he must lead a spade to forestall a possible squeeze in the black suits. It is true that if South has ♠ Q 10 the spade from East may cost an immediate trick, but this is no real danger, because if South holds Q 10 or Q 10 x of spades he is going to make the contract anyway.

The defender must work a little harder in a position of this kind:

```
            ♠ A K Q 7
            ♡ K 8
            ◇ Q 9 3
            ♣ 9 8 4 2
                N        ♠ J 8 4 3
                         ♡ 7
            W     E      ◇ J 10 8 2
                S        ♣ A K Q 10
```

South, who has bid hearts and diamonds, finishes in 3 NT. West leads a club and all follow to the Queen and King.

East knows now that he can cash four rounds of clubs. This will improve the declarer's timing, but the danger of not cashing the clubs is that South may be able to set up his ninth trick in hearts. So East makes the remaining clubs, South discarding one heart and West two hearts.

Now a switch to the Jack of spades is marked for two reasons: South, having bid the red suits and having turned up with three clubs, must hold a singleton spade, possibly the 10; and if a spade is not led at once, there will be a double squeeze, with spades as the pivot suit. The full hand is:

```
                    ♠ A K Q 7
                    ♡ K 8
                    ◇ Q 9 3
                    ♣ 9 8 4 2
    ♠ 9 6 5 2                      ♠ J 8 4 3
    ♡ Q 10 6 4 3                   ♡ 7
    ◇ 7 4                          ◇ J 10 8 2
    ♣ 7 6                          ♣ A K Q 10
                    ♠ 10
                    ♡ A J 9 5 2
                    ◇ A K 6 5
                    ♣ J 5 3
```

Now look at this deal, which was played in the semi-final of a big tournament at Las Vagas in 1972:

$\spadesuit$ Q 8 6 5
$\heartsuit$ Q 6 3
$\diamondsuit$ Q 3
$\clubsuit$ A Q 10 5

$\spadesuit$ K J 7
$\heartsuit$ A 9
$\diamondsuit$ A 9 8 7
$\clubsuit$ K J 7 4

$\spadesuit$ 10 9 3
$\heartsuit$ 2
$\diamondsuit$ K 6 5 4 2
$\clubsuit$ 9 8 6 3

$\spadesuit$ A 4 2
$\heartsuit$ K J 10 8 7 5 4
$\diamondsuit$ J 10
$\clubsuit$ 2

At a table where world champions Bobby Wolff and Jim Jacoby were West and East, West opened 1 NT (strong), South (the late Harold Ogust) bid Three Hearts, and North raised to Four Hearts.

A diamond lead is best, but Wolff opened the Ace of hearts and switched to Ace and another diamond. East won the second round and led the 10 of spades. Knowing that West held the outstanding high cards, South went up with the Ace and played off all the trumps. West, holding $\spadesuit$ K and $\clubsuit$ K J 5 in front of dummy's $\spadesuit$ Q and $\clubsuit$ A Q 10, was squeezed.

The editor of the American *Bridge World*, reporting the event, noted that Jacoby could have broken up the squeeze by the dramatic shift to a club into dummy's A Q 10. 'But it would have been one of the great defensive plays of all time', he added. Fie on you, sir! Anyone who had read this book would return the club 'in sleep'.